Crossway Bible Guide

Series editors: Ian Coffey (NT), Stephen Gaukroger (OT)
Old Testament editor: Stephen Dray
New Testament editor: Steve Motyer

Hebrews:
Crossway Bible Guide

Steve Motyer

Crossway Books Leicester

CROSSWAY BOOKS
38 De Montfort Street, Leicester LE1 7GP, England
Email: ivp@uccf.org.uk
Website: www.ivpbooks.com

First published 2005

British Library Cataloguing in Publication Data
A catalogue record for this book is available from the British Library.

ISBN-13: 978-1-85684-224-2
ISBN-10: 1-85684-224-X

Set in Palatino
Typeset in Great Britain by Avocet Typeset, Chilton, Aylesbury, Bucks
Printed in Great Britain by Cox & Wyman Ltd, Reading, Berks

To Sally Stiff and Brian O'Connor

In thankfulness for three weeks at Le Vernay
when Hebrews and the French countryside sang
joyfully to each other.

CONTENTS

Welcome!

These days, meeting together to study the Bible in groups appears to be a booming leisure-time activity in many parts of the world. In the United Kingdom alone, it is estimated that over one million people each week meet in home Bible-study groups.

This series has been designed to help such groups and, in particular, those who lead them. These Bible Guides are also very suitable for individual study, and may help hard-pressed preachers, teachers and students too (see 'How to use this Bible Guide', p. 11).

We have therefore enlisted authors who are in the business of teaching the Bible to others and are doing it well. They have kept in their sights two clear aims:

1. To explain and apply the message of the Bible in non-technical language.

2. To encourage discussion, prayer and action on what the Bible teaches.

All of us engaged in the project believe that the Bible is the Word of God – given to us in order that people might discover him and his purposes for our lives. We believe that the sixty-six books which go to make up the Bible, although written by different people, in different places, at different times, through different circumstances, have a single unifying theme: that theme is Salvation. This means free forgiveness and the removal of all our guilt, it means the gift of eternal life, and it means the wholeness of purpose and joy which God has designed us to experience here and now, all of this being made possible through the Lord Jesus Christ.

How to use this Bible Guide

These guides have been prepared both for personal study and for the leaders and members of small groups. More information about group study follows on the next few pages.

You can use this book very profitably as a personal study guide. The short studies are ideal for daily reading: the first of the questions provided is usually aimed to help you with personal reflection (see 'How to tackle personal Bible study'). If you prefer to settle down to a longer period of study, you can use groups of three to five studies, and thus get a better overview of a longer Bible passage. In either case, using the Bible Guide will help you to be disciplined about regular study, a habit that countless Christians have found greatly beneficial.

Yet a third use for these Bible Guides is as a quarry for ideas for the busy Bible teacher, providing outlines and application for those giving talks or sermons or teaching children. You will need more than this book can offer, of course, but the way the Bible text is broken down, comments are offered and questions are raised may well suggest directions to follow.

How to tackle personal Bible study

We have already suggested that you might use this book as a personal study guide. Now for some more detail.

One of the best methods of Bible study is to read the text through carefully several times, possibly using different versions or translations. Having reflected on the material, it is a good discipline to write down your own thoughts before doing anything else. At this stage it can be useful to consult another background book. See 'For further reading' on page 175. If you are using this book as your main study resource, then read through the relevant sections carefully, turning up the Bible references that are mentioned. The questions at the end of each chapter are specifically designed to help you to apply the passage to your own situation. You may find it helpful to write your answers to the questions in your notes.

It is a good habit to conclude with prayer, bringing before God the things you have learned.

If this kind of in-depth study is too demanding for you and you have only a short time at your disposal, read the Bible passage, read the comments in the Bible Guide, think round one of the questions and commit what you have learned to God in a brief prayer. This would take about fifteen minutes without rushing it.

How to tackle your group Bible study

1. Getting help

If you are new to leading groups, you will obviously want to get all the help you can from ministers and experienced friends. Books are also extremely helpful and we strongly recommend a book prepared by the editors of this series of Bible Guides: *Housegroups: The Leaders' Survival Guide*, edited by Ian Coffey and Stephen Gaukroger (Crossway Books, 1996). This book looks at the whole range of different types of group, asking what is the point of it all, what makes a good leader, how to tackle your meeting, how to help the members, how to study, pray, share and worship, and plenty of other pointers, tips and guidelines.

This book is a 'must' for all leaders of small groups. It is written by a team of people widely experienced in this area. It is available at your local Christian bookshop. If you have difficulty in obtaining a copy, write to Crossway Books, Norton Street, Nottingham NG7 3HR, UK.

2. Planning a programme with your Bible Guide

This guide is a commentary on God's Word, written to help group members to get the most out of their studies. Although it is never ideal to chop up Scripture into small pieces, which its authors never intended, huge chunks are indigestible and so we have tried to provide a diet of bite-sized mouthfuls.

If you want to get an overview of the Bible book in a series of meetings, you will need to select appropriate studies for each meeting. Read them yourself first and prepare a short summary of the studies you are tackling for your group. Ideally you could write it on a sheet of A5 paper and hand a copy to each member.

If you do not intend to cover the whole Bible book, choose a series of studies to suit the number of meetings you have available. It is a good idea to use consecutive studies, not to dodge about. You will then build up a detailed picture of one section of Scripture.

3. Preparing to lead

Reading, discussing with friends, studying, praying, reflecting on life ... preparation can be endless. But do not be daunted by that. If you wait to become the perfect leader you will never start at all. The really vital elements in preparation are:

▶ prayer (not only in words but an attitude of dependence on God: 'Lord, I can't manage this on my own')

▶ familiarity with the study passage (careful reading of the text, the Bible Guide study and any other resource books that throw light on it) and

▶ a clear idea of where you hope to get in the meeting (notes on your introduction, perhaps, recap what was covered at the last meeting, and what direction you hope the questions will take you in – don't force the group to give your answers).

Here is a short checklist for the busy group leader:

Have I prayed about the meeting?

What do I want to achieve through the meeting?

Have I prepared the material?

Am I clear about the questions that will encourage positive group discussion?

Am I gently encouraging silent members?

Am I, again gently, quietening the chatterers?

Am I willing to admit ignorance?

Am I willing to listen to what the group members say and to value their contributions?

Am I ready not to be dogmatic, not imposing my ideas on the group?

Have I planned how to involve the members in discovering for themselves?

Have I developed several 'prayer points' that will help focus the group?

Are we applying Scripture to our experience of real life or only using it as a peg to hang our opinions on?

Are we finding resources for action and change or just having a nice talk?

Are we all enjoying the experience together?

Setting the scene: Hearing Hebrews today

Hebrews is an amazing letter – if it *is* a letter. It doesn't begin with any opening greetings, unlike the letters of Paul, but it ends with them (13:22–25), and includes letter-like comments and instructions like 'Remember those earlier days … when you stood your ground in a great contest' (10:32) and 'Obey your leaders and submit to their authority' (13:17). Maybe there was once an opening greeting that has been lost – but at any rate, what is truly amazing is the *content* of this letter. At first sight, it looks rather complicated and distant from our perspective today. But once you get into it, it gets into you. Countless people have found that Hebrews becomes their favourite New Testament letter, once they get to know it. Some people become nuts about it.

Why? Because it presents a unique view of Jesus, and a unique understanding of the Christian life. There's nothing else like it in the New Testament. Only in Hebrews is Jesus presented as the 'great high priest' and compared with the mysterious Melchizedek (chapter 7). Only here are we told that he 'learned obedience' and was 'tempted' just like us (5:8; 4:15). Only here is his relationship to angels described (chapter 1). Only here is his entry into the heavenly sanctuary made the high point of his work for us, in comparison with the ritual of the Day of Atonement (chapter 9). And only here are we presented with the real possibility of losing our salvation (e.g. 6:4–6; 10:26–27).

That list has probably put you off completely. Yes, it seems strange at first sight. High priest … angels … Melchizedek … Day of Atonement – these are all unfamiliar ideas, seemingly far removed from life today. But they're worth working at, for several reasons.

1. We all need new ways of thinking, as Christians, to stretch us beyond our comfort zones and familiar patterns of thought. Hebrews certainly provides that.

2. More than any other part of the New Testament, Hebrews gives us a way of thinking about the Bible as a unity. Puzzled about how the sixty-six books of the Bible library hold together? Hebrews gives answers.

3. The difficult parts interlock with some wonderfully encouraging and inspiring sections, like the 'throne of grace' passage in 4:14–16, or the 'let us draw near' exhortation in 10:19–25, or the 'heroes of faith' gallery in chapter 11, or the 'two mountains' vision in 12:18–24. But we can't understand these properly apart from their context in this puzzling and powerful letter.

4. And finally, we really do need to know if it's possible to lose our salvation, or to think that we are saved but in fact deceive ourselves. 'Once saved, always saved'? Several books have been written with this title. But is it true? Is this what Hebrews teaches? Is it really different from what Paul seems to teach, for instance in Romans 8:31–39, where he tells us that 'nothing can separate us from the love of God'? This is a most important issue for us.

So be prepared for stretching of the mental muscles and development of your spiritual physique through studying this letter. You'll end up leaner, fitter, and better equipped to live with an understanding of your God, and of yourself, and better able to serve Jesus today.

As we shall see, the main argument of the letter involves a series of comparisons between Jesus and potential rivals, in the minds of the readers. In each case, the author wants to argue that Jesus is 'greater than' his rivals. A glance at the headings on the Contents page will show you how this works out.

Because we don't know who wrote Hebrews, I shall refer simply to 'the author', or to 'Hebrews', and assume that it was a 'he'. Some have wondered whether the author of Hebrews was a woman, and this is perfectly possible. But just for convenience I shall use 'he'. It would be nice to be able to use a name – and doubtless we would be able to, if the opening greeting had been preserved. But in the meantime – pending discovery in heaven – we shall have to say 'the author'.

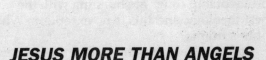

JESUS MORE THAN ANGELS

Hebrews 1 – 2

1:1-4

God speaks again

In a wonderful opening paragraph, the author of Hebrews introduces his cast list, and gives us a brief synopsis of the plot of this incredible drama.

The first four verses of Hebrews may have started life as a little hymn – they're worth singing, anyway. All the best worship songs are bursting with the best theology, and this is no exception. Who is on the cast of this drama?

God (1). He's the chief actor in Hebrews. He creates, speaks, promises, swears, forgives, judges, burns with fire, makes a new heaven and earth – and sits on a throne. Hebrews calls his throne 'the throne of grace' (4:16). He is the one, above all, to whom we human beings 'must render account' for our lives (4:13). Here, he 'speaks again' through his Son, breaking his silence since the days of the prophets.

The 'forefathers' (1). These are the ones God spoke to, before. Who are they? The author has in mind the whole nation of Israel, but perhaps especially the representatives who are going to appear later – the exodus generation (chapters 3 – 4) and the gallery of heroes in chapter 11, who cover the whole Old Testament story between them.

The prophets (1). These are the ones through whom God spoke. And they speak still, in this letter. There are about thirty quotations from the Old Testament in Hebrews, and lots more allusions – although in fact the whole argument of the letter hangs on certain crucial quotations, from Psalm 8 (2:6–8), Psalm 95 (3:7–11), Psalm 110 (5:6), Jeremiah 31 (8:8–12), Habakkuk 2 (10:37–38), and Proverbs

3 (12:5–6). The author takes 'the prophets' very seriously. They are still the voice of God.

The Son (2). Although God lies behind the whole story, 'the Son' is the chief character. He's the hero, who rescues the world from disaster. Others tried to save it – kings, priests, prophets, deliverers, the 'big names' of the Old Testament story – but they all failed. Only the Son, the greatest of all, wins through.

The angels (4). They might have saved the world, too – according to 1:14, God sends them to help people get saved. But they can tackle only bits and pieces. The whole job is just too big for them. The biggest job they undertake is *revealing the law to Moses*, according to 2:2.

No, the Son is the hero of the story. The author concentrates on introducing him, above all, in these verses.

Who he is. He is 'the radiance of God's glory and the exact representation of his being' (2). You could hardly ask for a clearer statement of the *deity* of Jesus Christ. Is it possible to distinguish between the glowing filament of a light-bulb and the light that streams from it? In theory, yes; but you can't have the one without the other. The glowing of the filament in the bulb is all part of the light it produces. Similarly, the word translated 'exact representation' points to the *inseparable unity* and *shared identity* of the Father and the Son – like the shape of a mould, and the thing moulded by it.

What he has done. He has 'made' two things here, on behalf of God. First he 'made the universe' (2), and then he 'made purification for sins' (3). The NIV translates the same Greek word with 'made' and 'provided', but I think we should connect the two statements. Two acts of creation, of equal scale and wonder! The author is going to concentrate on the second, in this letter. But the first one gives the second one its context. Because the Son is the one through whom God created all things, it is fitting that he is also the one through whom God *rescues* all things from sin. We're talking *cosmos*, here. Salvation in Hebrews is no fiddling little hole-in-the-corner activity, patching up people's faults. It's a remaking of the old order, as we shall see – a

21

whole rebuilding of humanity in a whole new creation. Nothing less will properly glorify the God who one day will shake the heavens and the earth, and bring in a 'kingdom that cannot be shaken' (12:26–28).

What he is doing now. Again, he is doing two things here – both in verse 3. He sustains 'all things by his powerful word'. And this is linked with his other activity; he sits 'at the right hand of the Majesty in heaven'. The 'right hand' is the position of authority, the place of the heir. God has appointed him 'heir of all things' (2), and he has 'inherited' the name of God himself (4). So now, raised to the position of 'heir', he sustains the creation, which he will one day inherit when it is finally made new.

This is worth thinking about. What keeps the world going? Scientists tell us that the universe runs *by its own momentum* – that its energy is within it, part of its own matter. There are three great forces or energies, they say – gravity, electromagnetism, and the forces that hold together the particles within the atom. But what generates these energies, holds them together, keeps them working in balance? We see the *effect* of that balance in the beautiful order of the world, the lovely rhythms of the weather, the fascinating reproductive cycles of countless animals and birds, the wonderful interdependence of the whole eco-machine – what a fantastic, amazing world we inhabit! And Hebrews says he *sustains* it. That simple word 'sustain' contains so much. It implies purpose: because he has also acted to 'purify' it, it will one day be remade, when he comes into his inheritance. So, in the meantime, he 'sustains' it, not allowing it to sink into dissolution and chaos.

'By his powerful word': just as the Father once spoke a 'word' to summon the universe into being, so now the Son's 'word' keeps it in being. The next time we hear his 'word' in Hebrews is in 2:12, where he says, 'I will declare your name to my brothers.' *We* are his brothers, and he reveals God to us. The glorious message of Hebrews is that the creator and sustainer of all things comes among us as a *brother,* to speak simply to us about his Father, and to bring us salvation.

Questions

1. If you are studying in a group, use the talents of the group to turn these verses into *an act of worship*, using music, words, drama, prayer, paint, whatever gifts you have.
2. Do the beauty and order of the world provide an argument for the existence of God? How would you reply to the objection that, if Jesus sustains the world, then he must be sustaining the life of murderers or rapists while they commit their crimes?
3. If God is the all-powerful creator and sustainer of his world, why has it been marred by sin? Imagine that you are writing to a non-Christian friend about this. What reasons will you give?

1:5–14

Jesus the glorious Son of God

Using a comparison with angels as the key, the author displays the wonderful glory and power of Jesus. Is he big enough, in our faith?

This is a powerful opening to the letter. The author collects quotations from 'the prophets' – in fact most of them from the Psalms – to prove that Jesus is greater than the angels. He introduces this idea in verse 4, and then pursues it through the rest of the chapter. It's still at the back of his mind in 2:16.

Why does he do this? Some people think that maybe the readers of Hebrews were being tempted to worship angels. There was a certain amount of this around, in the ancient world. Angels were thought of as mighty powers – almost like second-order gods – and people tried to tap their power. But there's no clear evidence that this was the problem the author is tackling – and actually he points to a different reason, in 2:2. There he accepts the Jewish belief that the law was revealed to Moses through angels. This belief rests on Deuteronomy 33:2–4, and we meet it also in Acts 7:53 and Galatians 3:19. So, if Jesus is *greater* than the angels, the revelation he brings must be *greater* than the law.

This fits with Hebrews' purpose. For reasons that appear as we go along, the writer wants to argue that *Jesus* must have absolutely top priority in his readers' loyalty. His word – the word that sustains the universe – takes precedence over all other revelations.

In the 'Digging deeper' section that follows, we will ask how the author is using the texts he quotes here. Let's concentrate now on what he draws out of them.

Verse 5; Psalm 2:7 and 2 Samuel 7:14: Jesus' unique relationship with God. Both these Old Testament passages are in fact about the king of Israel, who was thought of as having a unique Father–son relationship with God. Psalm 2 was probably written for his coronation, the day on which the new king heard God say to him, 'You are my Son; today I have become your Father.' No-one else in Israel had such a relationship with God – and no-one else in heaven, either. So also Jesus! He is uniquely 'the Son' of God, in an intimate *union of identity* with God, sharing his name (4).

Verses 6–9; Psalms 97:7 (Deuteronomy 32:43); 104:4; 45:6–7: Jesus' unique position on earth. This follows on. As God's 'firstborn', he deserves to share the worship reserved for God alone. The angels cannot be worshipped (see Revelation 22:8–9), but Psalm 97 apparently *commands* the angels to worship *him*! Then (verse 8) Psalm 45 actually calls him 'God'. This is the ultimate sharing of God's name – in fact, this is probably the 'name' the author has in mind in verse 4. Because he shares God's *name*, he also

therefore shares his *throne*. Psalm 45 wonderfully expresses the *joy* of this sharing. It was probably written for the
wedding of the king, but here in Hebrews the 'companions' are the angels, who rejoice to worship him. Jesus the
Son, sharing God's name, nature and throne, has been
anointed with the oil of joy beyond his companions (9).

*Verses 10–12; Psalm 102:25–27: Jesus' unique role in the
world*. This is the longest quotation in the list. In our
Bibles, these words were addressed to God himself, but
the author applies them without hesitation to Jesus. It may
be that, in his Bible, these words were addressed to the
Messiah (see the 'Digging deeper' section below). But
either way, the point is that Jesus the Son was God's agent
in creation (see verse 2), so he occupies the role of God
himself in relation to the world. 'They will perish, but you
remain ... your years will never end.' This is a note to
which the author will return at the end of the letter, as he
seeks to encourage his readers to *persevere* in their trials –
'Jesus Christ is the same yesterday and today and for ever'
(13:8).

*Verses 13–14; Psalm 110:1: Jesus' unique calling in God's
plan*. Verse 13 gives us the first quotation of Psalm 110,
which is a crucial psalm for the author of Hebrews. It's the
psalm that mentions Melchizedek – but the author is sav-
ing that up for chapter 7. Here we just get verse 1, which
is also quoted by Jesus in his famous exchange with the
Pharisees: see Mark 12:35–37. It could well be Jesus' use of
the psalm, applying it to himself, that prompted the
author of Hebrews to reflect on it more, and to develop his
amazing argument about Melchizedek.

When Jesus quotes it, he uses it to prove that the
Messiah will be *greater* than King David – David apparently calls him 'Lord'. Here, it's not just David but all the
angels who pale into insignificance beside the greatness of
Jesus the Son. This sequence of texts began in verse 3 with
Jesus at God's right hand, and that's where it ends, too:
but now it's not his position as *heir* that is underlined, but
his role as *victor* in God's campaign. His enemies are to be
made 'a footstool for [his] feet'. What campaign is this?

What enemies? The rest of the letter will tell us, though there's a hint here. He has won a victory that the angels, wonderful though they are, could not begin to achieve. They are simply 'ministering spirits' or 'spirits in the divine service' (14, New Revised Standard Version), sent out to do little jobs for the King, bits and pieces on behalf of 'those who will inherit salvation'. That's the big campaign – the winning of salvation, rescue, deliverance, restoration. The size of this job fits only one pair of shoulders – Jesus the Son of God.

Questions

1. What or who are the enemies that oppose the work of 'salvation' today – for you, your church, your society? How could you begin to see the power of Christ victorious over them?
2. Have you ever seen an angel? Are they still active? Should we believe in their activity still, and what could we expect from them?
3. Verses 8–9 talk about Jesus ruling in 'righteousness' – 'righteousness will be the sceptre of your kingdom'. But the world seems so full of injustice. How do we square our experience with what this passage teaches about the rule of the Son of God?

Digging deeper:
Old Testament quotations in Hebrews

You may have been a bit puzzled by some of the quotations in chapter 1. For instance, why does our author feel that he can just take verses written about the king of Israel and apply them to Jesus (Psalm 2; 2 Samuel 7; Psalm 45)? Or take verses addressed to God and redirect them to Jesus (Psalm 102)? We could just accept that he does this, and not regard it as a problem – but the fact is that he gives these verses a meaning very different from their original meaning. At worst, we could accuse him of pulling a fast one – of finding what he wants to find in verses that really say no such thing.

He does something similar with the quotation from Psalm 8, which we are about to meet (2:6–8). Originally, this is a 'creation' psalm, celebrating the position given to humankind in Genesis 1, as 'rulers' of creation. But he applies this, too, to Jesus. He is the 'real' meaning of this psalm, apparently.

Much has been written about the distinctive use of the Old Testament in Hebrews, some of it rather derogatory about the author's integrity. But actually there is a way of understanding what he does that makes sense, and that takes seriously both the original sense of these texts and their application to Jesus. It's a way of using the Old Testament that we find throughout the letter – we'll meet it again and again, so it's worth spending a moment explaining it here.

Let's take Psalm 45 as a first example (quoted in 1:8–9). It was a wedding psalm, written for the human king sitting on the throne in Jerusalem. But it says two things to him that were simply not true of any king there: 'Your throne, O God, will last for ever and ever.' It addresses him as God, and predicts that he will reign for ever. At the very least, we'd have to say that this is wishful thinking in the extreme. Similarly, Psalm 2 says hugely extravagant things about the king, immediately following the verse the author quotes (1:5): 'Ask of me, and I will make the nations your inheritance, the ends of the earth your possession. You will rule them with an iron sceptre; you will dash them to pieces like pottery' (Psalm 2:8–9). This never happened, either – neither for the great King David, nor for any of his descendants.

So the issue for our author is this: how can these texts be *rescued*, as God's word, from their non-fulfilment, or indeed untruth, in their original setting? His answer is to apply them to Jesus. It's as though he says: 'Yes, of course,

Psalm 2 and Psalm 45 were originally about the king in Jerusalem. But they use language about the king that was never true, and that therefore points beyond, to Someone Else – and that Someone we now find in Jesus! When applied to him, the promised Messiah-King, their language is true, and God's word through the prophets is vindicated.'

We shall see the author doing just this with Psalm 8, in the next chapter. As originally written, the psalm is simply untrue, because it proclaims that human beings are rulers of the whole world: 'you put everything under his feet' (Psalm 8:6). The author's comment on this says it all: 'At present we do not see everything subject to him' (Hebrews 2:8). Yes: we cannot control the seasons, the weather, epidemics; we're simply subject to the processes of growth and death that happen all around us. The author goes on, 'But we see Jesus, who was made a little lower than the angels, now crowned with glory and honour' (2:9). That's the point! Only the man Jesus Christ, who of course is the sustainer of all things (1:3), truly rules over the creation, and therefore *in his humanity* he rescues Psalm 8 as the word of God. And of course, as we belong to him, Psalm 8 becomes true for us, too.

We could illustrate this technique of our author with lots of further examples from later in the letter, but it's probably better to meet them when we get to them. His idea is to find the tensions, difficulties, and contradictions within the Old Testament Scriptures and to use these as pointers forward to Jesus. It's a brilliant technique.

It's worth pausing on one further issue. He always quotes from the Greek version of the Old Testament, known to us today as the 'Septuagint'. Perhaps he was a Greek-speaking Jew who didn't know Hebrew well, and so habitually used the Greek Bible. This causes some problems for us when the Greek Bible differs from the Hebrew one, which underlies all modern translations. For instance, neither Psalm 97:7 nor Deuteronomy 32:43 actually says, 'Let all God's angels worship him' (1:6). If you looked this verse up, you may have been puzzled. Also, there are some differences between the Hebrew and Greek versions of Psalm 102 that make it quite possible that our author read verses 25–27 as addressed to the Messiah, rather than to God.

Interesting! So the author of Hebrews treats as the inspired word of God a translation of the original Hebrew that differs from the Hebrew in quite a few respects. This is important, because it underlines to us that the Bibles we read, in whatever language, are God's word, and that God will affirm and use even bad translations. The Christian view of Scripture is very different from the Muslim view. For Muslims, only the original Arabic of the Qur'an was inspired. But for us, God's 'word' is not limited to a specific set of actual Hebrew and Greek words. And ultimately – as the author of Hebrews makes clear – this is because God's word is finally a *person*, Jesus Christ, 'in whom' God has spoken (1:2), and who alone makes sense of all the written words.

2:1–9

We see Jesus!

The terrible danger of 'drifting away' from faith is as real now as it was then. The author was deeply concerned for his readers – would he be worried about us too?

The second chapter of Hebrews is one of the most remarkable in the whole New Testament. We meet things here that are said nowhere else. And the author seems to mean it as a kind of introduction to the rest of his argument – he says many things here that are waiting to be unpacked later.

It begins with the first 'warning passage' (2:1–4) – the first of five passages in which the author warns his readers, very seriously, about the consequences of not persevering in their faith. (The others are 3:12 – 4:11; 6:1–8; 10:26–31; and 12:16–17, 25.) In fact, these passages together form the pastoral heart of the letter, the thing that really motivates it. If we were able to question our author directly, and ask, 'Why did you write this letter?', it seems that he would reply, 'Because I was so afraid that my dear friends were going to drift away from their commitment to Christ.' All the grand theology of the letter serves this practical, pastoral purpose. A 'Digging deeper' section on this topic follows, if you want to go into it more.

'Drift away' (1) is the term the author uses here to describe what he wants them to avoid – followed up with 'ignore' (3). He uses the same contrast that he developed in 1:1–4, between the old and new words from God. The consequences were terrible, if people drifted away from or ignored the old word, the law of Moses – how much more terrible if people ignore the new salvation? He doesn't specify what the consequences of 'ignoring' are: he just asks, 'How shall we escape?', which implies 'How shall we escape God's judgment?'

There's a great deal at stake here. To press home the significance of drifting away, the author lists the things that underline the greatness of this 'great salvation': 'the Lord' first 'announced' it – that is, the Lord Jesus. Then God confirmed it with 'signs, wonders and various miracles', and finally the Holy Spirit added 'gifts' of his own. So all three members of the Trinity were involved in the communication of this 'salvation'. Why might we want to drift away?

To cap it all, there's a contrast between 2:4 and 1:14. What help did people get from God under the old salvation? They got 'spirits', that is, angels sent to give occasional help. We know some of the angel stories in the Old Testament – angels appeared to Abraham, Jacob, Moses, Joshua, Balaam, Gideon, Manoah and his wife, and a few others. They hardly spread themselves thickly, and in all honesty they didn't do much. But what do we get under the new salvation? The Holy Spirit – one Spirit, but so much greater than angels. He comes to all, distributing gifts with great generosity. Why would we want to 'neglect' a salvation like this?

After this terrible warning – to be repeated later – the author plunges into his main argument. His start, in verse 5, is very surprising. God's concern, he says, is not with angels. He could have put them in charge of the world, but he didn't. Then follows the quotation from Psalm 8 that we considered above, in the 'Digging deeper' section on the Old Testament in Hebrews.

What's happening here? The author has two points that he wants to make with great passion:

1. *You are fantastically significant!* Human beings are far more significant to God than angels. When it comes to planning 'the world to come', the wonderful world that will replace this one, it doesn't cross God's mind to involve angels in the rulership. He has chosen human beings for that role. Psalm 8:6 says that he has put 'all things' under subjection to humankind – and the author takes 'all things' literally. He comments, 'God left nothing that is not subject' to human beings (8). For him, this includes everything that is yet to be, as well as everything that already is. Human beings truly are the pinnacle of God's creation, and he wants to share his kingship with us. See Romans 5:17 and Revelation 5:10 for parallel passages. We already see foretastes of this in the amazing technologies that exist today – ways in which God allows us to experience, even now, our rulership over creation, which will one day be perfected.

But of course it's so imperfect now! Technology is used to perfect war, and we do not control our destinies. The world strikes back with famine, floods, earthquakes, diseases. As we saw in the 'Digging deeper' section above, this is the key to the passage, for it leads to the author's second point.

2. *Jesus is fantastically significant!* Only in Jesus do we see what Psalm 8 was really saying. It seems ridiculous to describe human beings as 'a little lower than the heavenly

31

beings and crowned ... with glory and honour' (Psalm 8:5), when we see the degraded and wretched state of so many. Almost angelic? It's mockery to suggest this to the street kids of Rio de Janeiro. But *Jesus* came lower than the angels, and submitted to 'death for everyone', and because of that he is now 'crowned with glory and honour' (9). Brilliantly, the author reads 'lower than the angels' from a different angle – expressing not our dignity (almost angelic!) but Jesus' humiliation.

The contrast with chapter 1 could hardly be greater. Yes, we are talking of the same person – the 'Son' who is the heir of all things, through whom the universe was made. But he was 'appointed' heir of all things, sitting at God's right hand, *because* he 'provided purification for sins' (1:3). Now we begin to see what this means. He comes among us, 'lower than the angels', and dies for us.

Questions

1. Share experiences of 'drifting away' – yours, or those of others you know. What causes people to drift away from Christ?
2. 'We see Jesus' (9). 'Seeing' is an important theme in Hebrews. It's connected to faith – we 'see' by faith (11:13, 27). How do we 'see' by faith? What kind of 'seeing' is this? What does this passage suggest?
3. How can we convince people of their supreme significance and value as human beings? What difficulties stop people from seeing this?

Digging deeper: What's the problem?
Why Hebrews was written

It's the warning passages – the first of which we've just met – that make us ask about the reasons for the letter.

And since the warning passages are the places where the author suggests that we can lose our salvation, it seems very important to work out exactly what was happening with the first readers, and why the author was so concerned about them.

It seems pretty clear that the first readers were Jews. The Old Testament quotations, the interest in Old Testament topics and people, the throwaway references to 'our forefathers' in 1:1 and to 'Abraham's descendants' in 2:16, the author's concern to show how the two covenants, old and new, relate to each other – all this points to their Jewish identity.

It has often been suggested that the problem was that these Jewish Christians were thinking of giving up their Christian faith and going back to be 'just Jews'. And this seems to make sense, in the light of the warning passages and the author's expressions like 'drift away' (2:1), 'ignore' (2:3), 'turns away' (3:12), 'fall' (4:11; 6:6) and 'trampled the Son of God under foot' (10:29). But why would they want to do this – especially if they have received gifts of the Holy Spirit on believing in Jesus (2:4), really solid evidence of the reality of Christ?

It looks as though their group had quite a long history, too. They had leaders who have now died (13:7). They can look back on the beginning of their Christian life as a time of great trial, when they suffered persecution but came through victoriously: 'remember those earlier days', says the author (10:32). He reminds them of their care, at that time, for others imprisoned for their faith (10:34). What would prompt such a group to give up now?

As the first century wore on, things got progressively more difficult for Jewish Christian groups. They were required, more and more, to belong to *mixed* churches, of Jewish and Gentile Christians together. For some, this was very difficult, because they held scrupulous views about contact with unclean Gentiles. And as the Gentile mission was more and more successful, and the church became predominantly Gentile, Jewish Christians were pressed harder and harder by their fellow Jews to decide where they belonged. Are you Jews, or Christians? It became less and less possible to be both.

And often violence was involved, or at least threats of it. We can see all the issues in Acts 21, Luke's account of what happened when Paul arrived in Jerusalem, after an absence of many years. The Jewish leadership of the church there – especially James – were glad to welcome Paul, and rejoiced with him about the success of the Gentile mission (21:17–91). But then they warned Paul that many Jews in Jerusalem were deeply hostile towards him, having heard all sorts of wild rumours that he was telling Jews to abandon Moses. So they concocted a scheme – with which Paul went along – to convince people that he really was a law-abiding Jew. But it all went wrong, a riot ensued, Paul nearly got lynched, and the Roman garrison had to rush in to carry Paul out of the temple because 'the violence of the mob was so great' (21:35).

Luke does not comment on this, but we can easily imagine the tensions felt by Jewish Christians in Jerusalem at that time. They knew that James had welcomed Paul, and they too were glad that so many Gentiles had believed in Jesus. But they shared the concerns of their fellow Jews about Paul. Some may even have been willing to join the mob and denounce Paul as a law-breaker. But if they did this, they would be criticized by their fellow Jews for still being Christians, in theory on the same side as Paul. Very difficult!

We can imagine situations like this being repeated all over the Mediterranean world at this time – and we can also imagine that some Jewish Christians, under threat of persecution or simply because they had become disillusioned, decided to slip back into Judaism and to abandon the Christian bit of their faith.

We need to remember some vital factors here. **1.** Such Jewish Christians had never stopped worshipping in synagogues with their fellow Jews. They simply added 'messianic' worship (with 'charismatic' gifts) on the first day of the week. **2.** They still believed in the covenant with

Abraham and the reality of forgiveness under the old covenant. **3.** For them, therefore, belief in Jesus as Messiah was not a radical reorientation of religious belonging – it was more like the icing on the cake of their Judaism.

It all sheds a lot of light on 10:25, where the author says, 'Let us not give up meeting together, as some are in the habit of doing, but let us encourage one another.' Meeting together was the essential identity of the 'messianic' group on the fringe of the synagogue. If they stopped attending, then that in itself was the 'falling away' that the author feared. They would be saying, 'I'll just go to synagogue on the Sabbath. I won't persist with this Jesus Messiah stuff.'

This is why the theology of this letter is so vital. The author needs to convince them that Jesus is not the icing on the cake, but the whole substance and reality of the cake itself; that, apart from him, there's nothing; in fact, that they are quite mistaken in believing that there is still forgiveness of sins through Judaism. It's now available only through Jesus, him alone, greater than all.

That's the way into this letter for us. If we need encouragement to keep going when suffering comes, or our faith is being tested, or life is just tough – then let's stand alongside these Jewish Christians, the first readers of this great letter, and learn with them to keep our eyes on Jesus.

2:10–13

The heart of the matter

Now we begin to hear how 'such a great salvation' has been won for us.

For many centuries the 'official' view was that Paul wrote Hebrews, although there have always been doubts about this. But this just goes to show how little,  sometimes, 'officials' actually read their Bibles. It's quite impossible that Paul wrote Hebrews – not just because the author identifies himself as a second-generation Christian in 2:2 (Paul would never say this – see Galatians 1:11–12), but chiefly because Hebrews' understanding of 'the atonement' is so different from Paul's. ('The atonement' is the story of how God puts us right with himself.) It's not that they contradict each other – far from it. They just put things so differently. For Paul, Jesus' death and resurrection are the centrepiece of the work of atonement. The crucifixion and the empty tomb – these are centre frame for Paul. But here in Hebrews … well, let's look.

Hebrews 2:10–18 is a vital, condensed statement, to be unpacked at leisure as the letter unfolds. That's why we're studying it in two short sections. In verses 10–13 the author concentrates on who Jesus is, for us; in verses 14–18, on what he has done for us.

In verse 10 the author presents Jesus as 'the champion who leads many sons to glory'. This is a better translation than that of the New International Version (NIV) or the New Revised Standard Version (NRSV). Many have been inspired by the story of Gladys Aylward, who led a group of 100 orphans on a twelve-day trek to safety when China was invaded by Japanese armies in 1940. I remember hearing her preach, not long before she died, and thinking that she was certainly a powerful enough character to keep 100 frightened children going on such a terrible journey. That's who Jesus is, for us – our champion, leading us to glory, keeping us safe and confident on the way.

But what qualifies him to be the champion? Here's the most remarkable thing: 'It was fitting that God, for whom and through whom everything exists, should make the author of their salvation perfect through suffering' (10). If God is the creator of everything, couldn't he have just sent Jesus from heaven as a champion, already equipped with all the power needed to rescue us – to 'zap' the devil and whisk us off to glory? What's all this about being made perfect through suffering? The author doesn't explain yet – he simply says 'it was fitting'; and not in spite of the fact that God is the creator of everything, but because of it.

Verse 11 begins to explain. It should begin with 'For' (omitted in the NIV). A literal translation here would be, 'For both the one who sanctifies, and those who are sanctified, are all of one.' The translations try to unpack 'are all of one': the NIV has 'are of the same family'; the NRSV has 'all have one Father'. Hebrews is saying that there's an inner kinship between us and 'the Son'. We all belong together anyway, quite apart from the fact that he's God and we are human beings. Remember the statement, 'So God created man in his own image, in the image of God he created him; male and female he created them' (Genesis 1:27)? In Hebrews 2:11 the 'image of God' works backwards. In Genesis, it means that we are made like him. In Hebrews, it means that he is made like us. Because he is already 'of one' with us, bearing the same image, the champion cannot rescue us unless he actually comes to share our plight – to feel our pain, share our sorrow, experience our temptations, and die our death. Only so can he 'sanctify' us, that is, rescue us from sin.

Wow! What a thought! This is why it's *because* God is the creator of everything that Jesus must be made perfect through suffering. It's because he created us in his image, and therefore he cannot just zoom down from Planet Zog on a rescue mission and ship us out. Our pains are his – already. He's implicated in our plight. He will not stay distant from us, but will come and share all our woe.

He's our brother! You can sense the author's excitement as he introduces the quotation from Psalm 22:22 in verse 12. This of course is another Psalm of David, and is the one from which Jesus draws his terrible cry from the cross, 'My God, My God, why have you forsaken me?' After the agony of desolation, the last part of the psalm celebrates restoration – and the celebration is shared among brothers. That's the whole point. He's family with us, and he joins with us in praising God that he has been delivered (and we with him). A literal translation would be, 'In the middle of the church I will sing hymns to you.'

Now follow two really intriguing quotations from Isaiah 8:17–18 (verse 13). Once again, we're faced with the question: why does the author take these words, so special to Isaiah, and apply them to Jesus? This is the moment in Isaiah's story where, having been rejected by King Ahaz, Isaiah casts himself upon God and takes comfort in the fact that God has kept his promise, has given him children as he said, and is still speaking to Israel through his children. (Isaiah was told to give them names with a message.) Hebrews feels it's right to adopt Isaiah's experience and make it Jesus' experience too – because, after all, Jesus is 'family' with Isaiah, too, and is especially close to prophets. They, and he, are all charged with speaking God's word, as Hebrews has made clear in 1:1–4.

But Jesus' children are you and me. Whether his children, or his brothers, we belong together with him.

Questions

1. What do you think of the message of these verses? Spend a few minutes perhaps writing some reflections, or turning your thoughts into prayer. Be honest about any puzzles or questions you have.

2. 'I am trusting in him,' says Jesus through Isaiah's experience and words (see verse 13). On this view of the atonement, faith becomes something we share with Jesus. Examine your faith. What are you trusting him for? What do you find difficult to believe? Where do doubts attack your faith?

3. On this view of the atonement, again, our belonging to each other becomes a central part of the story. Our faith is shared with each other, as well as with Jesus. How deep is your 'brotherhood' with other believers? Do you share suffering with them?

2:14–18

Exactly like us

In one of the most powerful passages in the whole letter, we hear what Jesus has done for us, and why.

 This little paragraph concludes the author's summary of his message and opens up the way for the rest of the letter. It falls into two parts (verses 14–16 and 17–18), with the same structure to each part:

▶ A statement about Jesus being like us (verses 14a, 17a), followed by

▶ 'so that / in order that' – a statement of purpose (verses 14b–15, 17b), followed by

▶ 'for' – a statement of reason and motivation (verses 16, 18; the NIV has omitted 'For' at the beginning of verse 18)

Each part, though structured in the same way, has a different focus. Part 1 (14–16) has a *global* focus – Jesus as saviour of the world. Part 2 (17–18) has a *local* focus – Jesus as saviour of Israel. Having said this, however, all readers, whether Jews or Gentiles, are covered by both parts. It's just that the author uses some very special Old Testament language in Part 2, and here for the first time Jesus is introduced as the high priest.

Verse 14 summarizes the essence of verses 10–13 so movingly. Because of our kinship with each other, Jesus cannot be our champion unless he shares our 'flesh and blood'. The NIV introduces the word 'humanity', but this is a bit abstract. He shared *flesh and blood* with us. This is, after all, what God created – flesh and blood. He 'too' shared in the same things, says our author, using a strong word for 'too' that really emphasizes his full sharing of our fleshly condition. Nothing was left out when he became a man. The only thing missing was our sinfulness (see 4:15).

He shared it so that we might be saved from death. Here Parts 1 and 2 balance, because in Part 2 (verse 17) the purpose is to save us from sin. Death and sin are counterparts, the two terrible sides of our human condition. See how Paul connects them in Romans 5:12–14. They go together very closely, in the Bible, after being linked in the story of Eden (Genesis 2:17). We die because we are separated by our sin from God, the source of all life. But now Jesus is the source and giver of life, so when *he* comes in the flesh it's a different story. Now the power of death over flesh and blood can be broken.

The author mentions the devil in verse 14 – because if we are separated from God, then we come under the other awful rulership, that of the devil. The devil 'holds the power of death' – that is, he rules over the realm of death, the 'bottomless pit' or 'Hades', where the dead are kept (see Revelation 20:13). This is a realm to which all of us belong; we live under its 'fear', in a slavery from which we cannot rescue ourselves (15). From this slavery Jesus came to release us.

Verse 16 completes the author's concern with angels. They are immortal, like God; they need no saviour to rescue them from death. No – it's 'Abraham's descendants' who need that. There's real irony in this title, because to be descended from Abraham was the most wonderful thing for Jews. It meant that you were in covenant relationship with God himself – *not* separated from his love and power. But the author subtly points out that the old covenant – the covenant that starts with Abraham – does not in itself save us from the ultimate enemy, death. We *all* need this Saviour.

Part 2 goes over the same ground as Part 1, but expresses it so differently. Jesus was 'made like his brothers in every way' (17a), so that he might become a 'high priest' for us. This is the first mention of this great theme, which will be picked up again in 4:14 and then becomes the chief topic of the central part of the letter. The author leaves it unexplained at the moment. Why 'high priest'? He just hints at the answer here – the key to delivering us from death is dealing with our sins through offering a sacrifice of 'atonement for the sins of the people' (17). 'The people' here includes all of us, of course, but the author is using Jewish language to fit with the mention of Jesus as high priest. Israel is often called 'the people' or 'the people of God' in the Old Testament.

The chapter ends on a wonderful note. To be made like us in every way means that Jesus suffered – of course. The word translated 'tempted' here (18) also means 'tried' or 'tested'; it covers all sorts of trial. So Jesus bears all the same trials that we do. But his sufferings are as our high priest, the one who has come to save us. And so – the author puts it so simply – he is able to 'help' all who are going through trials of whatever sort. It can be physical suffering, arising from our 'flesh and blood'; or it could be emotional pain, like the fear of death; or it could be the consequences of our sinfulness – guilt, remorse, broken relationships; or it could be the powerful pressure of a temptation which we want to resist but can't. Whatever it is, he is 'merciful and faithful' (17), and is 'able to help' (18).

Looking back over chapter 2, we notice the huge emphasis on Jesus' humanity here. This really is the key thought for our author; this is the basis of the work of salvation. Jesus is completely human, like us in every way. But wait a minute – in chapter 1 there was a huge emphasis on his deity. Hebrews certainly wants to have it both ways: a saviour who is fully God, and fully human, and fully able to bring the two together for us, as well as for himself.

Questions

1. Turn the last verse into prayer, either for yourself or for others – or both. Who is facing trial at the moment, in need of the 'help' of Jesus?
2. What has been the most striking thing for you as you have studied Hebrews 1 and 2? Why did it mean so much to you? If you are studying with others, share your reactions.
3. For Muslims the thought of 'incarnation' is horrifying – they think that it demeans the dignity of God, and that it is completely incompatible with deity to propose that God can become a human being. How would you respond to this?

JESUS MORE THAN MOSES AND JOSHUA

Hebrews 3:1 – 4:13

Stop and look: The rescue mission

Now our author – how nice it would be to be able to give him a name! – sets out to develop the basic teaching he has already outlined, especially in chapter 2. His first step, in this next section, is to set Jesus' rescue mission into its biblical context, by comparing what Jesus has done with the other great rescue mission in biblical history, the one launched by Moses and Joshua. Jews, of course, believed that this was God's crucial intervention in Israel's history, in fulfilment of his promise to Abraham – the event that created the nation. They remembered it every year at Passover (as indeed they still do). Moses was tasked with the first part of the rescue, bringing the people out of slavery in Egypt. Then Joshua had the second job, bringing them across the Jordan into settlement in the promised land.

Our author's approach is radical in the extreme. Contrary to all Jewish tradition and sensibilities, he accuses Moses and Joshua of having *failed* in the task, so that conditions are ripe for Someone Else to do a better job. And then he tells the readers … well, read on!

The son and the servant

A radical contrast between Moses and Jesus: Jesus is far greater, so he is the focus of God's rescue plan for his people, not Moses.

The author's first move is to encourage his readers simply to think about Jesus (1).

He calls them 'companions in a heavenly calling'. Sadly the word 'companions' has disappeared in the NIV, which is a pity, because it is significant. The NRSV has 'partners'. It appears again in 3:14, where the author really says, 'We are the companions of Christ, if we hold our confession firm.' This is the same word that was used in 1:9, about the angels who are 'the companions' of the Son of God in the heavenly rejoicing about his status as son and heir. A beautiful relationship is possible for us, here. We can be drawn into 'companionship' with Christ, as well as with each other, sharing a 'call' to enter the rejoicing of heaven itself.

But the key to it is to think about Jesus – to consider who he is, to 'fix your thoughts' on him. That's really the author's whole message, in fact. Everything hangs on thinking clearly and rightly about Jesus. If he can get his readers to do that, he will have achieved his purpose.

So this process of comparison and contrast between Jesus and Moses is vital. This will help them to clarify their understanding of Jesus. Having been introduced as a 'merciful and faithful high priest' in 2:17, Jesus is now described by the key word 'faithful' (2). ('Merciful' becomes the key word in the next section – see 4:16.) Moses was 'faithful in all God's house', and similarly

Jesus was 'faithful to the one who appointed him' (2).The author is actually quoting the description of Moses by God himself in Numbers 12:7, where Moses is also called 'my servant'. The point in that passage is to distance Moses from other so-called prophets, to exalt his status and make him very special. I reveal myself in dreams and visions to others, God says, 'but with him [Moses] I speak face to face … he sees the form of the LORD' (Numbers 12:8). So the description of him as 'my servant Moses … faithful in all my house' (Numbers 12:7) makes him unique among Old Testament prophets.

But, great though Moses is, Jesus is greater. He is not a 'servant in' God's house, but a 'Son over' it (6). His absolutely unique relationship with God ensures that there is no comparison, really. The greatest Old Testament prophet bows and leaves the stage.

What is 'God's house' here? This is a subtle symbol, with three layers of meaning, all of them significant here. First, 'God's house' was Israel, the nation – and this is the primary meaning in Numbers 12. 'The house of Israel' is quite a frequent expression (see, for instance, Hebrews 8:8). And because Israel is his chosen people, this 'house' belongs to God. Secondly, 'God's house' was the temple, the special place of his presence. Because the worship of the tabernacle and temple are so significant later in Hebrews, I'm sure it's right that we find this hinted at here, too.

And thirdly, God's house was the universe. This meaning appears in Solomon's prayer of dedication of 'God's house' in 1 Kings 8:27: 'But will God really dwell on earth? The heavens, even the highest heaven, cannot contain you. How much less this temple I have built!' From this thought, various Jewish writers at the time of Hebrews had developed the idea that the whole cosmos is God's temple, his proper dwelling-place. The author reveals that he has this meaning of 'house' in mind in verse 4: 'For every house is built by someone, but God is the builder of everything.' This fits with how Jesus has been portrayed in chapter 1. He is the builder of everything, on behalf of his Father. Hence he is 'the son over the house of God', the ruler of the whole world.

This is why the author writes as he does in verse 3: 'Jesus has been found worthy of greater honour than Moses, just as the builder of a house has greater honour than the house itself.' When it comes to building 'houses' for God, Jesus can knock the socks off anyone, especially Moses. In fact, Moses was *part of* the house – merely a 'servant' within it. So Jesus has far greater 'honour' – and therefore deserves far more attention, and *thought*, than Moses.

That leads the author to his conclusion in verse 6: 'we are his house, if we hold on to our courage and the hope of which we boast'. We are his house – we are back to the 'people of God' meaning now. God's intention always was that he would 'indwell' his people, just as he 'indwelt' the temple and 'indwells' the cosmos – the use of the term 'house' for all three is not accidental. But the crucial point here is that believers in Jesus become the 'house of God', the people who belong to him, provided they don't back away from the deal and resign their membership.

The final blow is struck in verse 5. The purpose of Moses' servanthood, says the author, was to testify 'to what would be said in the future'. Apparently, the only really significant thing about Moses' ministry as a prophet was that he testified to the coming of Jesus. Forget all the laws, forget the Ten Commandments, forget all the legislation that set up the sacrificial system – Moses' crucial prophecy is in Deuteronomy 18:15, 18, where he predicts the coming of a 'prophet like me', about whom God says, 'I will put my words in his mouth, and he will tell them everything I command him.' These are the things that 'would be said in the future' – the revelation to be brought later by the 'Son' through whom God now speaks (1:2). Far more important than Moses!

Questions

---

1. Is it God, or Jesus, who figures more largely in your prayer life and Christian life generally? How Jesus-centred is your spirituality? Share your thoughts about this with others.
2. If Jesus is so much more significant than Moses, why do we still bother with the Old Testament? What would the author of Hebrews say to this?
3. Does it really make sense to think of Jesus, the exalted Son of God, as ruler of the cosmos today? How do we square this with the terrible things that happen in the world?

3:7–19

A dangerous journey

The author takes his readers by surprise by comparing them to the rebellious exodus generation, who failed to enter the promised land.

'Journeying' is a great theme in Hebrews. In fact, it's the chief picture of the Christian life, as we shall see especially in chapters 11 – 13. We're on the move, travelling hopefully, drawing near to Mount Zion (see 12:18–23), our eyes set on Jesus (12:1–3) – except that it's awfully easy to get distracted, lose direction, stop, and miss out on the goal. John Bunyan's famous *Pilgrim's Progress* is an excellent book to read alongside Hebrews, because it develops the same picture, and is very real about all the snares that can trap us and stop us from getting to the Celestial City. Jesus is on the move, too, as we shall see, and our journey is essentially following him where he has gone before.

So the journey of the 'children of Israel' from Egypt to the promised land provides a great picture for the author of Hebrews, and he develops it by a long quotation from Psalm 95 (7–11). His choice of this passage reveals his anxiety about his readers – it's a warning to the contemporaries of the psalmist not to copy the exodus generation, and thus ruin everything by falling into unbelief.

The introduction to the quotation is fascinating (7): 'So, as the Holy Spirit says ...' The present-tense 'says' shows that the author thinks of these words as addressed to the 'Hebrews' (and us) right now, by the Holy Spirit. Had this text been specially 'given' by the Spirit at one of their worship gatherings – perhaps when the author was with them? Or maybe, by these words, the author is expressing his own Spirit-given awareness that this text applies specially to them. (See 9:8 for another example of Spirit-given teaching.) This looks ahead to his description of the 'word of God' as 'living and active' in 4:12: the Scriptures are not dry-as-dust religious texts from ancient times, but the living, *present* word of the Holy Spirit to us.

Having said this, however, the author is not ignoring the original setting and reference of the psalm. In fact, these are vital for his argument. These words were spoken by God about a group of people exactly like the 'Hebrews' – he details the comparison in the next section (especially in 4:2–3). And so they need to take very seriously the terrible fate that befell them. Exactly the same thing could happen again.

We can see how the author applies the quotation in verses 12–19. They – and we – need to guard against becoming unbelieving and rebellious, and hardened by sin's deceitfulness, every single day (12–13). The 'today' of the quotation in verse 15 – its first, emphatic word – means that, on this journey, not a day must pass without checking up, and guarding against 'rebellion'. The reason for this is in verse 14, 'We have come to share in Christ *if* we hold firmly till the end the confidence we had at first.' The 'if' in the middle is emphatic – it should stand out in bold print, or italics, as here. This is staggering; we have come to share in Christ (past tense) *if* we go on maintaining our confidence in him (in the future). So what we have done in the past is radically affected by what we will do in the future.

This might seem illogical or even impossible. If I've taken a degree course, for instance, then that's part of my past, whatever I do in the future. I'll always be entitled to put 'BA Hons' (or whatever) after my name, even if I never make specific use of it. Some people think like this about a decision to believe in Jesus – it's always there, tucked away in the past, giving security and eternal life. Once saved, always saved. But in Hebrews, the journey picture makes it all look different. You can set off from Cape Town fully intending to travel to Johannesburg – but unless you actually keep going and arrive there, your intention on leaving Cape Town is worth nothing at all. It doesn't give you any letters after your name.

The last part of chapter 3 is very sobering. The author really rubs home his point with a series of three questions, picking up different words in turn from Psalm 95, and making precisely this point.

1. *Who heard God's voice and yet rebelled?* The whole exodus generation (16). Hebrews is referring to the dreadful incident in Exodus 17:1–7.

2. *With whom was God so angry?* With all the sinners, 'whose bodies fell in the desert' (17). This refers to Numbers 14:26–35, where God pronounces judgment on Israel and tells them that none of those who left Egypt will enter the promised land except the two spies, Joshua and Caleb, who believed that God could give them victory after crossing the Jordan. All the rest will 'fall in this desert'.

3. *To whom did God swear that they would not enter his 'rest'?* All those who disobeyed (18). This too picks up the language of Numbers 14 (verse 22).

The punchline in verse 19 says it all: *unbelief* robbed them of their goal. And you, says the author, are in exactly the same danger.

Questions

1. This is sobering and difficult to read. Does our salvation really depend on whether we keep going or not? What about 2:10, and the picture of Jesus as our champion, 'leading' or 'bringing' us to glory? How much depends on his leading, and how much on our following?
2. The Israelites sinned many times on the journey before the final crunch point described in Numbers 14. God forgave them for their earlier sins – but there was something different, apparently, about that last episode. What was it? Why didn't (or couldn't?) God forgive them again?
3. Turn this passage into prayer for yourself, and for people you know who started the Christian journey, but have left the road. And ask: what was it that drew them away? What could make *you* stop?

4:1–11

Entering the 'rest'

The author continues the challenge. He doesn't want the 'Hebrews' to miss out. We mustn't miss out either on the 'rest' God plans for us.

'Resting' and 'travelling' are incompatible. By definition, when we rest, we stop whatever activity we were involved in, whether travelling, working or playing.

And there is a wonderful rest waiting at the end of the journey for all who persevere and don't give up en route. In this passage the author expounds the last verse from his quotation of Psalm 95, 'So I declared on oath in my anger, "They shall never enter my rest"' (3:11). He develops the idea, asking, 'What exactly is this "rest", from which they were excluded?', and he finds the answer to his question in Genesis 2:2. Once again, it's a gripping and very challenging argument. Here are its four main steps.

1. Remember, he says, that the exodus generation, who so tragically missed out, were exactly like you. They had 'the gospel preached' to them, just like you. But because they didn't believe it, they lost out. If they had believed, they would have entered 'God's rest' – this was what he swore to exclude them from (1–3).

2. So we can conclude that if we believe, we too will 'enter the rest of God'. What is this rest? Genesis 2:2 tells us – it's the 'rest' that God himself enjoyed when he had finished his journey through creation and laid down his tools after six days' hard work (4–5).

3. When can we enter this rest? The psalm says 'today'. This was written in the time of David, long after Joshua – so the invitation was being held out then, to David's contemporaries. This just confirms that Joshua did not give the people 'rest' as promised (6–8).

4. So a 'Sabbath-rest' is still on offer, to the people of God. We can still go in, and rest from hard labour as God did – but it needs effort to get there! We still need to heed the warning example of those who could have entered, but whose disobedience prevented them (9–11).

There's much to think about here. It's a condensed argument, flitting around the Old Testament. The reference to Joshua giving them 'rest' in verse 8 picks up the many references to this idea, such as Deuteronomy 12:10, 'But you will cross the Jordan and settle in the land the LORD your

God is giving you as an inheritance, and he will *give you rest* from all your enemies around you so that you will live in safety.' See also Deuteronomy 25:11; Joshua 11:23; 14:15; 23:1 – it was a frequently expressed idea, referring to the political and social peace that Israel expected to enjoy in the promised land.

But ... along comes Psalm 95, written long after the conquest under Joshua, recording God's oath that they would *not* enter his rest, after all. Looks like a contradiction! – except that things like this are meat and drink to our author. When he finds tensions or contradictions of this sort, he exploits them. If the Scriptures are God's word, such things must be deliberate. So he hunts around for reasons, especially reasons that make Jesus the answer to the riddle. (See the 'Digging deeper' section on his use of the Old Testament, pages 26–29 above.) In this case, he develops two points out of the contradiction, both vital for his argument.

1. If Joshua didn't give them rest, then God must have been promising more than just 'political security and peace'. Yes, he was – Genesis 2:2 shows us that he was offering a sharing of his own private rest, a really special fellowship with himself.

2. If Joshua didn't give them this rest, then – if the offer in Psalm 95 is real – the invitation must be still open. What God wanted Israel to have, when he led them out of Egypt, was entry into his own life. But they never entered it. Yet Psalm 95 implies that it's always possible to resist hardness of heart, and to 'hear his voice' – it can be done 'today', any day. So 'there remains a Sabbath-rest for the people of God' (9)

This is a difficult passage to understand. The essence of it lies in what the author means by God's *rest*. It's God's own private life, what he does with his time off, his relaxation time – the time he wants to share with friends at the end of a busy week creating. Who does he have round? He

53

invites the people he's most fond of, the people he can trust, and who trust him. In fact, there's a standing invitation for people like that – 'Saturday at God's – come and chill!' This is because faith is a relationship, not just a condition of mind. People who trust God like to be with him, and he with them. It brings us together.

When do we enter this rest with him? The end of the journey sounds like heaven – do we just enter it when we die? There's a 'Digging deeper' section on this at the end of this study – suffice it to say that, for the author of Hebrews, it's always possible to 'draw close' to God, and to enjoy intimacy with him.

Questions

1. 'Let us, therefore, make every effort to enter that rest' (verse 11). How do we do this? This sounds like 'salvation by works', doesn't it? – getting into relationship with God by our own 'effort'? What kind of 'effort' is this?
2. Do you think it's really true that the Israelites, at the time of the exodus, had heard the same gospel as the one we believe (verse 2)? What is the core common to the message they had heard and the Christian gospel? You may need to discuss this one with others – but it's a very important question, because the unity of the Bible is bound up with it.
3. Take the 'today' very seriously. What do you need to do, today, to respond to God's call on your life?

Digging deeper: Christians and 'the Sabbath'

When the author says, 'There remains, then, a Sabbath-rest for the people of God' (4:9), he doesn't mean that Christians must keep observing the Sabbath! This 'remaining' is something much grander and more wonderful, as we have seen – a sharing of God's own personal rest, in an intimate relationship with him.

However, he uses the word 'Sabbath', and this raises a important issue for us. There's a real puzzle here. Keeping the Sabbath (the seventh day of the week, Saturday) as a day of rest is one of the Ten Commandments – the fourth (see Exodus 20:8–11). But Christians don't obey it, even though we would be the first to insist that 'You shall not murder' (no. 6) or 'You shall not commit adultery' (no. 7) are vital for today.

Christians never have obeyed this commandment, apart from groups such as the Seventh-Day Adventists who define themselves by their literal keeping of it. Traditionally, many Christians have transferred the Sabbath commandment to Sunday, the Christian day of worship, thus making Sunday a compulsory day of rest on which no work may be done. I grew up in such circles. When I was a child, on Sunday we were not even allowed to buy an ice-cream, because this was causing the ice-cream seller to break the commandment. But we were never told why we were obeying the Sabbath command a day late! The transfer of the Sabbath commandment on to the Christian Sunday affected the shape of the week in most western countries, with shops and businesses still largely closed on Sundays. In Britain the 'Keep Sunday Special' Campaign has fought to keep Sunday as a day of rest, when workers are not compelled to work. But it is interesting that the arguments used to support 'Keep Sunday Special' have been social, not biblical: not that it's against God's law, but that it undermines family life and leads to people being exploited by demanding employers.

So where does the truth lie, and how does Hebrews help us to understand the meaning of 'Sabbath' for us today?

The reasons why Christians have never kept the Sabbath are not hard to find. The first Jewish Christians met on Sundays as well as the Sabbath, to celebrate their new messianic faith together – in fact, this is probably what the 'Hebrews' were doing. The first day of the week was the day of resurrection. Then, as the church became predominantly Gentile and separated from the synagogue, Christians met only on the first day – usually, it seems, either at dawn, or late in the evening, because many were slaves who could not take a whole day of rest (see Acts 20:7; 1 Corinthians 16:2).

But behind this practical, historical reason lies theology. The apostle Paul insisted that 'we are not under law, but under grace' (e.g. Romans 6:15). He taught that the law must be filtered through Christ – we are first and foremost 'under the law of Christ' (1 Corinthians 9:21; Galatians 6:2), and if Old Testament law fits with obedience to Christ, then we accept it. As a 'day of observance', the Sabbath came in a package with the Jewish festivals (Passover, Tabernacles, etc.) and with other specifically Jewish customs such as circumcision, and so Christians did not feel that they had to keep it. Nowhere does the New Testament command Christians to observe it.

Hebrews might seem to support this complete dropping of the Sabbath commandment as irrelevant for Christians. At first sight, the Sabbath is 'spiritualized' in Hebrews – that is, its spiritual significance is sought, as a symbol of sharing God's 'rest', his life and presence. It would be perfectly possible to say, 'But we should be sharing God's rest – in so far as we can, this side of heaven – every day, and not just one day per week.' And this must be true.

But at the same time, the Sabbath command is grounded in the creation itself, not just in Genesis 2:2, which Hebrews quotes, but also in Exodus 20:8–11. There we're told to rest on one day per week, because God made the heavens and the earth in six days, and then rested on the seventh. There's a pattern here, a rhythm balancing work and rest. Yes, it's true that Jesus 'worked' on the Sabbath, and said that he was reflecting God's Sabbath-work in doing so (John 5:15–18). He insisted that it was God's will that we should do good on the Sabbath (e.g. Mark 3:4). So 'resting' doesn't mean *inactivity*. But it would surely be a strange way of responding to the invitation to share God's rest if we then made no difference between Sunday and the rest of the week, or spent all days exactly alike. At the very least, there's a rhythm of work and play to be discovered, which may be different for each person because our lives are under such different constraints.

But for all of us, what would be the marks of 'Sabbath' in our lives? We need times of celebration, when we stop and look around, as God did at the end of creation 'and saw that it was very good' (Genesis 1:31). We need times of re-creation, when we rest and let body, mind and spirit recharge their energies. And we need times of service, when we give ourselves to doing specific good in the Lord's name, as Jesus did – ways of balancing the 'secular' week with direct service for the Lord. Such times, especially if focused on one day, will help us to realize the goal of 'entering God's rest' more and more in our lives.

4:12–16
Naked! But not ashamed

In this 'crossover' passage the author first terrifies us, then comforts us. We have a truly fearful and wonderful God.

Yes, this is a 'crossover' passage, because it covers the movement from the second main section of the letter (3:1 – 4:13) into the third, which is really the whole central part (4:14 – 10:39). See 'Stop and look' on pages 61–62 below for details. We could say that verses 12–13 conclude the last section, and verses 14–16 begin the next – and this would not be untrue, but it wouldn't be the whole story. The 'Therefore' in verse 14 gives the game away. It's looking back at what has gone before, and responding to it, drawing a conclusion. In particular, it is responding to verses 12–13, and that is why it makes sense to study these five verses together.

These two little passages – separated by a large paragraph division in many translations – are two of the most quoted passages in the Bible. They contain such vivid imagery, first about 'the word of God' (the sword that divides), and then about Jesus the high priest and the 'throne of grace'. But, taken separately, we miss their force. Taken together, they are overwhelming.

The first passage is deeply challenging, if not downright depressing. Here 'word of God' has a double meaning. On the surface, it's referring back to the quotation from Psalm 95 that the author has been expounding for the last chapter. He finished with an encouragement to 'be eager' to enter God's rest. How do we know when we're 'eager'? Or eager enough? The word of God faces us with the challenge not to harden our hearts. But we know that our hearts are hard – terribly hard, and rebellious. Is there any hope? By issuing us with the challenge, and by reminding us of the terrible story of the Israelites whose bodies fell in the desert because their hearts were hard, the word of God cuts into our hearts too.

The author develops this picture of 'cutting'. God's word is like a sword, he says, that doesn't just cut but also dissects, like a scalpel. It can probe into us, revealing our inner workings far more clearly than we are aware of them ourselves. Who can distinguish clearly between the soul and the spirit? Who can say where one ends and the other begins? In my own devotional reading at the moment I am enjoying *The Interior Castle* by St Teresa of Avila, the great sixteenth-century mystical writer. More than anyone else in the tradition of Christian prayer and mysticism, I think, she probed the inner workings of the soul. But she confesses again and again that she doesn't fully understand how soul and spirit relate to each other. And she is deeply aware of her own sinfulness. Modern 'depth psychology' also tries to work out how we are constructed, interiorly. But there's no agreement! Some psychologists even deny the existence of a 'spirit' within us.

But God's word makes a demand of us that tests our motivations to the very depths. How can we be sure of our 'eagerness' in responding to him when we don't understand ourselves, and have no idea what mixed, sinful, corrupt or rebellious instincts may be working deep inside us?

And that brings us to the other meaning of 'word of God'. It doesn't just refer to Psalm 95, but more generally to the word of judgment that God speaks over us. His two-edged sword pierces our very depths, and 'judges the thoughts and attitudes of the heart'. He doesn't just know what's really there, he judges it. Then the thought of judgment is developed in verse 12 – it's as though we are naked before him, completely exposed, and required to 'give account' to him for what he exposes in us. The word translated 'laid bare' contains the image of the 'neck on the block'; before this sword, it's as though we are tried, convicted, and already on the scaffold, waiting for the executioner's blow. How can it be otherwise? How can we be different from the exodus generation, who had it all, and threw it away?

Praise God for verses 14–16! The 'Therefore' is wonderful, because it connects this desperate picture with all that the author has said about the rescue mission launched by Jesus. Apart from him, we are completely lost. But we don't have to be 'apart from him'. We can 'have' him – the very first word in verse 14 (literally, it's 'Having, therefore, a great high priest ...'). Our chief task, therefore, is not to discern the complex workings of our hearts and souls, but to 'hold firmly to the faith we profess' – that is, to our relationship with Jesus and our confession of him. Why is this the vital thing to do? The author gives two reasons, in verses 15 and 16.

First, *because he sympathizes* (15). What a verse! It's not just that he discerns what goes on in our hearts far more clearly than we do; he's experienced it all himself. He's been there, because he shares our flesh and blood (2:14). He knows all about mixed motives, weak faith, complex desires, sexual distraction, repressed emotions, physical pain, bereavement, unfulfilled longings – you name it, he's felt it from the inside, 'yet was without sin'. By the power of the Spirit, he lived a sinless human life in flesh and blood, in unbroken fellowship with his Father.

Secondly, *because he helps* (16). High priests give access to special places – we'll discover all about this in the coming chapters. This high priest gives us access to 'the throne of grace', the place where God is. Isn't this the place from where he stabs his sword into us, exposing our wretchedness? Yes, but that's not his only action towards us. In fact, that's not the action that counts, if we are willing to 'draw near' through our high priest. Then we discover that he is a God of 'grace', willing to show 'mercy' and to give 'grace to help us in our time of need'. These words are so simple, but so marvellous. Even those deep needs, the things unknown even to us, that cause us to wake in the night, full of fear – even in relation to those there is 'grace', 'mercy', and 'help' for those who 'draw near'. We can come, not shrinking and afraid, but 'with confidence' (another great Hebrews word). How can we hang back?

Questions

1. Teresa of Avila had a famous vision in which she saw an angel with a golden spear tipped with fire, which 'he plunged into my heart several times, so that it penetrated to my entrails. When he pulled it out, I felt that he took them with it, and left me utterly consumed by the great love of God.' Turn this 'sword' passage into prayer, asking for the penetrating and healing power of the grace of God in your heart.
2. Did Jesus really experience every single temptation that we feel? What about the special temptations associated with old age, since he died young?
3. Should we help one another with our temptations, or is it better to deal with them privately before God? If we support one another in dealing with temptations, what's the best way to do it?

Stop and look: The central part of Hebrews: Jesus more than Aaron (4:14 – 10:39)

This is the third 'more than' section in Hebrews: we started with the angels (chapters 1 – 2), then moved to Moses and Joshua (chapters 3 – 4), and now come to Aaron, the first high priest. Someone has pointed out that Hebrews deals with these 'more thans' in descending order of power, starting with the most powerful. If Jesus is greater than the angels, then he must surely also be greater than Moses, and Aaron. This was important for the 'Hebrews' to whom this letter is addressed, because they were still members of their synagogues and took an 'icing on the cake' view of Jesus. He was a great addition, as Messiah, to all that they already had as children of Abraham. And what they had was particularly associated with the figures of Moses and Aaron: Moses, the great deliverer and revealer, who had secured the nation's existence and the renewal of the covenant, and Aaron, the great legislator, who had set up the whole religious life of Israel with its worship rituals and festivals. For all practical purposes (because he had the greater impact on everyday life), Aaron was the more significant of the two, and so he receives the longer treatment in Hebrews. Jesus is 'more than' Aaron!

This long central section has a distinct pattern to it:

A 4:14–16   First exhortation to 'use' our high priest
  B 5:1–10   Introduction to Jesus as high priest: looking ahead the whole central section
    C 5:11 – 6:12   First warning, based on the message of Jesus as high priest
      D 6:13 – 7:28   Jesus as high priest, Part 1: in relation to Abraham and the old-covenant promise
      D' 8:1 – 10:10   Jesus as high priest, Part 2: in relation to Jeremiah and the new-covenant promise

B' 10:11–18 Summary of Jesus' high-priestly ministry, looking back to the introduction in 5:1–10

A' 10:19–25 Second exhortation to 'use' our high priest

C' 10:26–39 Second warning, based on the message of Jesus as high priest

There's a basic ABCD–DCBA pattern here, which is not unusual in the Bible. Bible writers were very careful with the structure of their writing. But you'll notice that the sections are a bit swapped around at the end – this is because the author wants to finish with the warning passage (10:26–39). This is really where his whole pastoral concern is focused, and he wants it to flow out of the great theology of this part of the letter, and the exhortation to 'use' our high priest that precedes it.

On either side of this central section, we have the people of the old covenant – the terrible negative example of the exodus generation (3:7 – 4:13), and the wonderful positive roll-call of the 'Honours List' in chapter 11. On either side of that, the exhortation to 'fix your thoughts on Jesus' in 3:1–6 and 12:1–4. And on either side of that, we have sections that emphasize our 'family' union with God, through Christ, using the language of parenthood, brothers and children (2:10–18; 12:5–13).

So Hebrews is very carefully put together. And in this third section we are in for a treat, as the author takes us through a dramatically different presentation of what Jesus has done for us – different from anything else in the New Testament. Our study of it will not only deepen our love for Jesus, but also give us a glorious sense of the unity of God's salvation plan, in Old and New Testaments.

For ease of presentation, we're going to divide it into two parts in this *Bible Guide*, 4:14 – 7:28, and 8:1 – 10:39. As in miniature in 2:14–18, the first part concentrates on who Jesus is, and the second on what he has done.

JESUS' APPOINTMENT

Hebrews 4:14 – 7:28

Digging deeper:
Making sense of 'priesthood' for today

Before we get into the detail of the presentation of Jesus as high priest, it's worth pausing to think about the problem this raises for us as we apply it to ourselves today. The difficulty is that 'priests' have a very bad press today. We have all been shocked by the exposure, in recent years, of the sexual abuse of children carried out by various Catholic priests. At the same time a few Muslim imams and other clerics have gained a terrible reputation for openly advocating hatred and inciting their followers to violence. In the secularized West, people do not feel the need for any 'priest' to help them. In Protestant churches, 'priest' is not a preferred title for the 'minister' or 'pastor' who leads the church. Only in Catholic and Orthodox churches are 'priests' still in charge, although even here the distinction between 'the priesthood' and 'the laity' has been considerably broken down in recent years.

How can we communicate 'Jesus as high priest' so that it connects with people's needs today – or indeed with our own needs? It is helpful to ask what function priesthood fulfilled in the Old Testament, as a background to finding answers to this. Essentially, the priest was the vital go-between, mediating between the people and God. The interface between the realm of God on the one hand, and the realm of this world on the other, was a dangerous place. If you strayed into God's presence accidentally, you could get killed. Yet we all need God. Especially in Israel, people knew that their whole identity as a people depended on their relationship with God. How can connection with the divine be regulated, controlled, kept safe? The answer was the priesthood: a group of men (no women involved), tasked with the tricky business of managing the contact between God and his people, without incurring harm either to themselves or to the people.

There were very strict rules about how this was to be done, as we shall see. The rules were for the protection both of the priests themselves and of the worshippers who 'drew near' to God. At the heart of their work was the 'sacred space', the physical point of intersection between this world and the realm of God. Ordinary worshippers could not approach this space, but the priests could – and right into its heart went the high priest, just once a year, on the Day of Atonement. As he and the other priests worked in and around the sacred space, they functioned as representatives of the people. Because they were there, the people were there. And representation also worked in the other direction, too: the priests represented the presence of God among the people, and could be channels of revelation from him.

So 'representation' is the key idea in priesthood. And unlike priesthood, representation is a very current idea today. It's very important in politics, with representatives likewise mediating between the people they represent and the focuses or sources of power (the political 'sacred spaces' of today). It's important too in art, with different schools of art all trying different ways of presenting or representing truth or reality, and certain artists becoming famous as special representatives of particular approaches. It's important in medicine, as the great practitioners mediate their expertise to the sick, representing the hope of health. For many people, psychotherapists are the secular priests of today, because they mediate deliverance from psychological disease, the secular equivalent of 'sin'. And representation is extremely important in popular culture, where various 'pop idols' stand for or represent what many people aspire or long to be. Some celebrities are like high priests of their own cult, with adoring followers trying to imitate them as much as possible. In all these ways representatives are seen as mediators of something important, something that we feel is vital for our lives, without which we cannot live.

That's the way into understanding Jesus as high priest. Keep the word 'representative' in mind. He stands for us, and he stands for God. In that supremely dangerous area, where life and death collide, he can forge a path that we can then tread safely after him. He represents true humanity, as we have already seen – human life lived as well as it possibly can be. And he represents God, as well – true deity shown among us, not hidden away behind veils where it cannot harm. It is he who reveals to us that God sits on a throne, not of power or vengeance or justice, but of grace.

That's Jesus, our high priest. It's vital to tell his story, the story of his life, because it's through his story that people begin to be able to connect with him today. And, as we'll see, that's what Hebrews does, too.

5:1–10

Jesus our great high priest

The author of Hebrews at last explains why he is so keen to describe Jesus as 'high priest'. And we discover how important is the Garden of Gethsemane.

The first verse of chapter 5 follows straight on from the exhortation to 'approach the throne of grace' in 4:16 – because in biblical thinking you need a priest if you are going to draw near to God (see the 'Digging deeper' section immediately above). The author has told us that Jesus is that high priest for us (2:17; 4:12) – now he begins to explain what kind of priest he is, and how his priesthood works.

This passage makes three points about priesthood, and applies them all to Jesus. The points are made in general, about all priests, in verses 1–4 , and are then repeated – in reverse order – in application to Jesus in verses 5–10. Here they are in verses 1–4:

1. Priests are appointed from among human beings, and as a result can sympathize fully with human weaknesses (1a, 2). Their humanness means that they are prey to the same weaknesses themselves.

2. Priests have the job of offering sacrifices for sins on our behalf (1b). As noted above, they have the difficult job of managing 'matters related to God', a potentially very dangerous thing to undertake – especially since their weaknesses mean that they have to offer sacrifices for their own sins as well as ours (3).

3. Priests don't appoint themselves; they are appointed by God (4). Put alongside point 1, this shows how they represent both sides – both us and God. This is what happened to Aaron – see God's words of appointment in Exodus 28:1.

Now these points are applied to Jesus, with the exception, of course, of the qualification added to point 2, that he needs to offer sacrifice for his own sins also. The author reverses the order.

3. Jesus was appointed by God to this role (5–6) – and, says the author, this is precisely what is implied by the verse from Psalm 2 that I quoted about him in 1:5. 'You are my Son; today I have become your father' – this is the language of appointment. In chapter 1 it was appointment as king. Here, it is appointment as priest. In fact, he occupies a unique office, that of priest-king, combining both roles. Which is what Melchizedek did. The author drops a trailer for chapter 7 by mentioning Melchizedek for the first time, quoting the basic verse around which chapter 7 will revolve, Psalm 110:4. As we shall see, Melchizedek was both a king and a priest, and this combination of roles is essential for Jesus' ministry. This sets him apart from Aaron and his sons. He

rules the universe as its king, and stands alongside us as our priest.

2. He offers sacrifices (7) – here, the sacrifice of his agonized tears and cries in the Garden of Gethsemane. This is clearly what the author is referring to – see Matthew 26:36–46. The language Hebrews uses here is very strong, emphasizing the agony Jesus went through as he faced death, and using the technical word for 'offering up' a sacrifice. Jesus knew that a terrible 'cup' was approaching, which he would have to drink. He cried 'to the one who could save him from death', that is, God his Father. And then Hebrews adds, 'and he was heard because of his reverent submission'. This does not, of course, mean that he was delivered *from* death. God heard his prayer, and saved him *through* death, or *after* it. For our author, the tears of Jesus in Gethsemane are the focus of his sympathy with us, the point where our priest most aligns himself with our pain, and our plight. For we too shrink from death in fear; remember 2:15, where 'fear of death' is the thing, above all, from which we simply cannot deliver ourselves as human beings. Jesus steps into that fear and feels it himself, and out of that fear prayers arise as sacrifices before God.

1. He was appointed from among us. This follows on, and the author focuses on it in verses 8–10. Here he makes some remarkable statements. As one of us, and like us, this Son of God 'learned obedience from what he suffered', and thus having been 'made perfect' he was 'designated' by God to the Melchizedek priesthood, and 'became the source of eternal salvation for all who obey him'. Wow! He truly is one of us, if he went through the same process of growth and learning that we do. It's true for us, too, that we learn most through the things we suffer. And that process of very human suffering and learning – focused on the experience in Gethsemane – was what led God to 'designate' him as high priest.

A 'Digging deeper' section comes next, looking into these ideas a bit more. But just let the drama and wonder of these thoughts soak into your mind and feelings about Jesus. He is the Son through whom the worlds were made (1:2), and yet, 'although he was a son' (8), he goes through a very human process of growth and development through suffering. Can you get your head around that? You can certainly turn it into praise!

Questions

---

1. How essential is suffering to being human? Is it just a nasty side-effect of life in a fallen world, or is it the essential context of human sympathy and love? Could we develop the fruits of the Spirit (Galatians 5:22) *without* suffering? See James 1:2–4.
2. Do you think that we can have a 'priestly' ministry towards each other, or is Jesus' priestly ministry unique? If he's the high priest, can there be subordinate 'priests'? See 1 Peter 2:4–10.
3. What have you learned through suffering in your life, or in the lives of others? If you are studying in a group, share some testimonies with each other about this.

Digging deeper: Jesus 'learning obedience' and 'being made perfect'?

Hebrews is dramatic. The Son of God, who made everything (1:2), learns obedience through suffering and is 'made perfect' (5:8), and therefore becomes the source of salvation for all who follow him. This mind-blowing story could make the headlines of any newspaper (if editors would listen).

But how do we understand it? Surely the agent of creation was not lacking in perfection, and did not need to learn something? In what sense, therefore, did he 'learn' and 'become perfect'? Those who think and write about these things have offered four possible explanations.

1. *The 'journey's end' idea.* This theory says, 'Let's retranslate "made perfect".' It doesn't carry the idea of overcoming faults, and achieving moral perfection, but of overcoming obstacles, and achieving a destination. This view picks up on the prominence of the 'journeying' picture in Hebrews and applies it to Jesus. So 'made perfect' in 5:8 would mean 'reached his destination in heaven, seated at his Father's right hand'.

This view is worth considering. It's true that the verb translated 'made perfect' can sometimes have this idea of reaching a goal. But that's not its usual meaning. And here in Hebrews we have to reckon with the fact that not only Jesus but we too are 'made perfect'. See, for instance, 10:14, where it would be very difficult to limit the notion of 'made perfect' to 'reach a goal'. There, it's in parallel with 'be sanctified'. It could be translated 'become mature', rather than 'be made perfect', but maturity is more than just reaching a developmental destination; it involves qualities. It's likely that this maturity or perfection happens to us in the same sense that it happens to Jesus – because this is the vital parallel that Hebrews draws: what happens to him happens to us, too.

2. *The 'ordination' idea.* It's really interesting that, in the passages in Exodus and Leviticus that describe the ordination of Aaron and his sons, the verb 'make perfect' is used in the Septuagint (the Greek version of the Old Testament that the author of Hebrews uses) to describe their 'ordination' to office. For instance, in Exodus 29:9 and Leviticus 4:5 the Hebrew expression 'fill their hands' is translated 'perfect their hands'. ('Fill their hands' signified giving them the tools and tasks of their office.) Is this what it means in Hebrews 5:8 and 2:10? (See also 7:28.) Again, it would not be a matter of introducing a missing moral perfection, but it would be another way of saying that God appointed him to the office of high priest.

This is an attractive idea, and it would be hard to deny

that this is part of the meaning, because it fits so nicely with the parallel between Aaron and Jesus. But again, as a total explanation, it fails to consider the parallel between Jesus' perfection and ours. The word is used three times of Jesus (2:10; 5:8; 7:28), and six times of us: three negative (7:19; 9:9; 10:1), and three positive (10:14; 11:40; 12:23). We must seek a meaning that covers all nine references.

3. *The 'vocational' idea.* This view is a bit broader than the 'ordination' view. It says that Hebrews' whole interest is in the office and ministry that Jesus fulfils. The author is not really concerned about Jesus' inner life, but about what he achieves as the appointed priest-king who dies for his people. So when Hebrews says that 'he was made perfect through suffering', it means that his suffering enabled him to be the perfect priest – to be exactly what we needed, to fulfil his 'vocation' or calling to save us.

Again, this is an interesting approach, and is undoubtedly right. The problem is not in what it says but in what it doesn't say. We can't help asking: how did suffering enable Jesus to be the perfect Saviour? And, rather than saying simply, 'Because it was his vocation to die on the cross, to be our Saviour', Hebrews says, 'Because through suffering he learned obedience.' Hebrews goes further than this view recognizes – Hebrews does make comments about Jesus' inner life, especially in 5:7–8.

4. *The 'personal growth' view.* This approach seems the best, in fact, mind-blowing though it is. It says that through his incarnation and his sharing of our flesh and blood, and through the suffering that this entailed, the Son of God learned a new obedience to his Father. It was part of his humanity to do so – because we all learn to know and love God better as we go through suffering. Hebrews will say this very clearly in 12:5–11. The Son of God is no exception, because his humanity is exactly the same as ours. So he goes through personal growth, like us, moving into a deeper knowledge of his Father, and it is this process – this growing in obedience through his experience of flesh and blood – that qualifies him to be our high priest.

71

This is truly staggering. Through the incarnation, we can say, a permanent change is introduced into the being and nature of God himself. The Son of God is changed by it, and so, therefore, is God in his wholeness. This change is hinted at in the Preface (1:1–4), although it's really just a puzzle at that point. We need the rest of the story to explain it. How can the one who is the very expression of God's own nature (3) actually become something else (4)? Or how can the one who made the world become its heir (2)? Puzzling – until we read the story of the incarnation, and of the growth of the Son of God as one of us. He was tempted, tested, tried in every way, just like us!

5:11 – 6:12

Don't be 'sluggish'

The author opens his heart in this first really intense 'warning passage'. We hear how he really feels about the Hebrews, and what he really longs for them to experience.

This passage begins and ends with the same word, translated by the NIV as 'slow to learn' in 5:11 and 'lazy' in 6:12. The NRSV has 'dull in understanding' and 'sluggish'. It would be helpful if the translations used the same expression in both places, because clearly it sums up for the author what he feels about the Hebrews. It's the sort of word that must have been used frequently on school reports in ancient Greece! It combines the ideas of poor understanding and poor commitment. You can see how useful this word nothros would have been for teachers – it could go in several categories on the report. We have to think of a pupil who just can't cotton on to what the teacher is saying, and as a result ends up gazing out of the window.

In fact, I think the author is subtly teasing his readers in 5:11–14. He has given them some intense and difficult teaching up to this point, and he has just made a throw-away reference to Melchizedek, one of the most obscure characters of the Old Testament, as if everyone would know without difficulty what he meant. Now he says, as if to tantalize them, 'It's all been so easy so far. I could give you crowds of really fantastic teaching on this, but of course you're not ready for it yet.' But if he is teasing them, behind it lies serious concern. He is deeply worried that his readers are losing their commitment to Jesus – gazing out of the classroom window because they think they're in the wrong lesson.

There are actually some hotly debated issues in this section of the letter, and, rather than try to set out alternative (or rival) views, I'm simply going to outline the way of looking at it that makes sense to me, after much study of it.

The 'Hebrews' are Jewish Christians tempted to give up meeting with the 'messianic' group on Sunday mornings (10:25) and to continue just with their membership of the synagogue. They believe, in any case, that the Abrahamic covenant is fully valid. If we were to put them on the spot and ask, 'Do you think that your fellow Jews will be saved at the judgment day, even if they haven't believed in Jesus?' they would probably say, 'Of course! Why not?'

But the author, although a Jewish Christian himself, has come to a very different view of Jesus. Jesus *is* essential to salvation. There is no longer any salvation to be received through the Abrahamic covenant, or through Old Testament worship. But he doesn't want to attack the old covenant head-on. If he did this, he would lose his readers immediately. They would certainly skip class next time. He wants to persuade them that he is right – to tempt them into his viewpoint by excellent theology. This is why he begins with Jesus and his unsurpassed greatness – because that's what it all hinges on, in fact.

73

This passage is where he gets the most direct with his readers. We need to move on to perfection and maturity, he says (6:1). There's so much more to be learned! As yet we've only scratched the surface of all that is to be gained from knowing Jesus. Let's leave behind the basic foundations that you learned in the synagogue, the basic teachings about the Messiah, about repentance, about faith, about ritual washings (baptisms) and other ceremonies (laying-on of hands), and about the things to come, resurrection and eternal life (6:2). These are just the basics, learned by every Jew or Gentile convert to Judaism. We need to press on beyond these basics.

And there's a great deal at stake here (the author goes on), for once you've repented before God by believing in Jesus, and received the forgiveness of your sins through him, and begun to enjoy all the other blessings that come from faith in him (listed tantalizingly in 6:4–5), then there is actually no further effective repentance for you within Judaism. If you decide to give all this up and be 'just Jews', then you are effectively re-crucifying Jesus, because you are aligning yourself in membership with the community that decided to execute him rather than receive him. Don't do that! For within Judaism there is no longer an effective repentance – how could there be, if Jesus is the high priest? If he's been shut out, how can there be forgiveness of sins by exclusively 'Jewish' repentance? Make sure that you produce a good crop for God, blessed by him, and not a crop of worthless works that he will curse (7–8)!

The author finishes his exhortation by calling them 'beloved' (9) and telling them that he is sure they won't do anything so foolish. You've done so well in the past – and indeed in the present (10), he says. Keep going – don't give up! 'Imitate those who through faith and patience inherit what has been promised' (12) – and here he looks forward to chapter 11. The saints of the old covenant will show them what to do!

This reading of these verses makes a lot of sense in terms of the situation of the first readers, which was something very particular. They had learned to enjoy charismatic gifts and the power of the Spirit, including miraculous healings (6:4–5), but they were still tempted to give up and become 'just Jews' because of their faulty theology. Or, we should say, because of their faulty Christology – their inadequate view of Christ. The author wants to assure them that, now that Christ has come, there is no going back to the ways things were before.

Questions

1. Can we lose our salvation, or is it 'once saved, always saved'? This is such an important question. (There's a 'Digging deeper' section below on it.) Doubtless you can think of people who once called themselves Christians and perhaps were very active in the church, but have now slipped away from commitment to Jesus. Does this passage teach that they can never come back – they can't 'be brought back to repentance'?
2. How good are our churches at giving people 'solid food' as Christians? How could it be done better – and what kind of teaching do you think counts as 'solid food'?
3. 'Imitate' (6:12). Example is so powerful. Reflect on those who have inspired you in your Christian discipleship. What was it about them that you found so encouraging? Share testimonies with others if possible.

Digging deeper: Can we lose our salvation?

The passage we've just studied (6:1–8) seems to say, not only that we can lose our salvation, but, even more soberingly, that, once it's lost, we can't get it back. 'It is impossible for those … to be brought back to repentance …' This seems to fit with Hebrews 10:26, which says that 'no sacrifice for sins is left' for those who keep on sinning deliberately, and with 12:17, where the example of Esau is given: 'Afterwards, as you know, when he wanted to inherit this blessing, he was rejected. He could bring about no change of mind, though he sought the blessing with tears.' It seems as though he repented but his repentance was not acceptable. This does not sound just or merciful – surely God would not turn away any sinner who repents, however terrible their sin? We could even cite the parable of the prodigal son as such an example (Luke 15:11–32). The younger son had it all, and threw it away – but his Father welcomed him back with open arms into the same family he'd rejected. Isn't our God like that?

We shall look at 10:26 and the story of Esau in due course. Perhaps the best way to tackle this issue is through a series of questions and answers.

Can you lose your salvation through occasional sins? No, of course not. God is so merciful.

Can you lose your salvation through a single, terrible sin – like the unforgivable 'blasphemy against the Holy Spirit'? Jesus certainly says that that particular sin cannot be forgiven (Mark 3:28–30), though he emphasizes in the same place that every other sin will be forgiven. David committed adultery and then secretly murdered the woman's husband – a terrible, premeditated sin. Yet he was forgiven the instant he repented (2 Samuel 12:13). Clearly, 'blasphemy against the Holy Spirit' must be something truly dire.

Can you lose your salvation through repeated, terrible sins – habitual, deliberate flouting of his will? I suppose this is like asking whether God would have forgiven David if he'd made a habit of committing adultery and murdering the unfortunate husbands. Something like this is in mind in Hebrews 10:26, where it's continual and willing sin that is in mind. But even there a special factor is operating, as we'll see – the author is referring to the sons of Eli, who were priests at Shiloh, where the tabernacle was pitched before the temple was built. They abused their position by exploiting people, stealing offerings and having sex with the serving girls, and they refused to change when Eli rebuked them. Because they 'were treating the offerings of the LORD with contempt' (1 Samuel 2:17), and thus 'blasphemed God' (3:13), it was said that there could be no sacrifice for their sins (3:14). The point is that they were in a very special position, charged with the holy things in the holy place, ministering on the threshold of the very presence of God. This is probably what is meant by the 'blasphemy against the Holy Spirit' – the Pharisees were warned against this (not charged with it) when they accused Jesus of performing exorcisms by satanic power. In the special presence of the Holy – the Holy One, the Holy Spirit – special conditions apply.

If Jesus tells us to forgive each other an unlimited number of times (Matthew 18:21–22), then it's unlikely he operates by different rules, however dreadful our sins may be.

Can I lose my salvation by finally and irrevocably rejecting Jesus? Yes. Hebrews clearly says this.

If someone I know has done this, should I conclude that they can't come back and regain their salvation? How do you know that their rejection is final and irrevocable? You'd need to be able to predict the future. God will surely welcome all repentant sinners, but those who have once been insiders will find it much more difficult truly to repent and believe. They need lots of love and care. I would never conclude that it's all over for anyone. In Hebrews 6:6 it would be better to translate '*while* they are crucifying the Son of God all over again', rather than '*because* they are crucifying …'; as long as they persist in their rejection of Jesus, then of course they cannot be restored. But what if they begin to change their mind about him?

What about Esau, then? Wasn't the door barred against him returning? We'll look at him when we get there. (Or you can sneak a preview now – Hebrews 12:15–17.)

Is 'once saved, always saved' untrue, then? Hebrews certainly denies this old slogan, because of its emphasis on the journey of faith. Salvation in Hebrews is a destination, not a ticket – it's the terminus, not the bus. So if we decide to give up and never actually arrive, then by definition we won't have arrived.

Can I never be sure of my salvation, then? Should I always be worried that I won't make it? No, this is not what the author of Hebrews teaches, because of his confidence in God and in Jesus as high priest. Later in chapter 6 he says that God has promised salvation and confirmed his promise with an oath, so that 'we who have fled to take hold of the hope offered to us may be greatly encouraged. We have this hope as an anchor for the soul, firm and secure' (6:18–19). And then he identifies the 'hope' with Jesus. But this is the security of those who know that they have a completely reliable guide on the journey, one who will take every step to keep them safe. We can trust him 100%!

We could summarize it like this. Hebrews understands salvation relationally, not mechanically. But our instinct is to understand it mechanically, rather than relationally. In other words, we feel that if we've been 'saved', something has 'happened' to us; God has flipped a switch, installed new software, germinated his seed in us – and because this action and its consequent change are past, how can they be undone? Something has happened to our 'mechanism' which means that we are for evermore 'saved'. But the author of Hebrews, and indeed the rest of the Bible too, does not think in these mechanical terms. Salvation is the result of the relationship between the high priest who goes before and the people who follow. If the people live in that relationship, they are saved. If they renounce or even just 'ignore' it (2:3), they can't be.

But this doesn't mean insecurity. My parents have been married for fifty-six years. Now nearly eighty, they could no more renounce or neglect their relationship with each other than fly to the moon. They are secure in their love for each other – they've become symbiotic, grafted into each other as people. In theory, they could fall out with each other and divorce, but really we know that this is impossible. Salvation is for those who stick to Jesus and become symbiotic with him, whose lives are oriented around him even when the relationship is difficult.

Soul anchor

The author prepares to introduce Melchizedek by bringing in the theme of the promise to Abraham. This is the basis of our 'hope', as Christians.

At first sight it looks as though a major section in the argument begins at 7:1, with the focus on Melchizedek. Many translations put a strong paragraph break there. But no – this is actually misleading. Verse 13 of chapter 6 marks the beginning of the next main section of argument, after the author's encouragement to the readers to move on from basics to mature teaching. They need to reassess their whole understanding of Abraham and their relationship to him; this is part of the mature teaching they need to grasp.

Paul does something similar in Galatians 3 and in Romans 4 – he looks at Abraham through new eyes, from a Christian perspective. Paul's angle was that he wanted to show how Abraham is the 'father' of Gentile believers in Jesus – a revolutionary new way of reading the Abraham stories, showing Jesus as the 'seed' to whom the promises were made, so that all who are 'in' Jesus by faith are also 'Abraham's seed, and heirs according to the promise' (Galatians 3:29).

But Hebrews' take on the same issue is very different from Paul's. Whereas Paul quotes the promises to Abraham in Genesis 15 and 17, Hebrews moves on to the later story of the sacrifice of Isaac (Genesis 22:1–19). This is the source of his quotation in verse 14 (he actually quotes Genesis 22:16–17). This story was very famous among Jews, as the single great act by which Abraham earned the favour of God and became established as the father of the nation. And it is certainly true, as Hebrews points out, that this is the point at which the earlier promises are confirmed with an extra oath: 'I swear by myself, declares the LORD, that because you have done this and have not withheld your son, your only son, I will surely bless you and make your descendants as numerous as the stars.'

This story was also especially significant, because Jews thought that it anticipated the sacrificial system established later under Aaron. Abraham's sacrifice of his son was stopped, at the last second, by the appearance of a ram to take his place. The key words 'ram', 'burnt offering', and 'appear' or 'be seen' all come in the story (Genesis 22:7–8, 13, 14), and the only other place where they all occur together is in Leviticus 16, the Day of Atonement chapter (Leviticus 16:2, 5, 24). Jews believed that it was through the provision of the sacrifices, and of the festivals such as the Day of Atonement, that the enjoyment of the blessings promised to Abraham in Genesis 22 was guaranteed to his children. And, remarkably, this is the chapter to which the author of Hebrews refers at the end of this passage when he says that Jesus, our hope, has entered 'behind the curtain' (19). The phrase 'behind the curtain' is taken from Leviticus 16:2, 12, from the instructions given to Aaron about how to conduct the Day of Atonement (when the high priest makes his annual entrance into the Most Holy Place 'behind the curtain').

The author wants to make a link between the promises to Abraham and Jesus. He wants to show how Jesus is the essential fulfilment of the Abrahamic promises. How does he do it?

First, he underlines the absolute security of God's promises to Abraham. This is the point of the oath, explained in verses 16–18: the 'two unchangeable things' in verse 18 are the promise (that Abraham would be the father of the chosen nation) and the oath by which the promise was secured.

Secondly, he identifies himself with all who still want to

take refuge under the promise to Abraham. This is in the second half of verse 18, where he writes about 'we who have fled to take hold of the hope offered to us'. The last two words here, 'to us', are not actually in the Greek; the NIV has supplied them. And in fact it would be better to supply 'to him', referring to Abraham. 'We' take hold of the hope offered to Abraham. The author is thinking, of course, especially of Jews and Jewish Christians like himself.

Thirdly, he then links the Genesis 22 promise to Abraham with the sacrifices prescribed by the law, especially the Day of Atonement. This is in verse 19: the promise to Abraham is our 'hope', the sure anchor of our souls, because it opens up the way into the presence of God himself, as on the Day of Atonement.

But then, fourthly, he takes his readers by surprise by linking it dramatically to Jesus in verse 20: Jesus is our forerunner, who has entered behind the veil like the high priest on the Day of Atonement. He did so because he was a high priest in the order of Melchizedek, says our author – thus leaving us panting for further explanation.

Hebrews deliberately, and cleverly, keeps the name of Jesus to the end. And describing him as our forerunner is staggering: no-one ever expected to follow the high priest into the Holy of Holies on the Day of Atonement. He was definitely on his own, and entered on behalf of the whole nation. But Jesus, apparently, intends that we should follow. This must be something to do with his being a 'Melchizedek' high priest. Again, we wait for explanation.

So, all in all, we are fully prepared for the next chapter. This will show – we hope – why Jesus is the fulfilment of the promises to Abraham. The author recruits Melchizedek on to his team to help him do it.

Questions

1. Why did God command Abraham to sacrifice his son Isaac (Genesis 22:1–19)? What can we learn from this

story for ourselves today? Note Paul's dramatic allusion to the story in Romans 8:32.

2. Hebrews says here that Abraham 'received what was promised' (15), but in 11:13 he comments that Abraham 'died in faith without having received the promises' (NRSV). How do you explain this? Can we 'receive' promises in different ways?

3. Remind yourself of some of the promises of God, the ones that are specially important for you now, or have meant a lot to you in the past. Share your thoughts with others. Which promises are you trusting particularly, and why?

7:1–10

Meet Melchizedek

Like Abraham himself, we meet one of the strangest biblical characters – stranger than fiction. But in his uniqueness he points forward to someone even more significant.

Peter Jackson's wonderful film of *The Lord of the Rings* has recently been released to critical acclamation all over the world. And it is indeed a superb rendition of J. R. R. Tolkien's gripping trilogy. But one thing 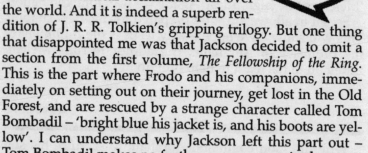 that disappointed me was that Jackson decided to omit a section from the first volume, *The Fellowship of the Ring*. This is the part where Frodo and his companions, immediately on setting out on their journey, get lost in the Old Forest, and are rescued by a strange character called Tom Bombadil – 'bright blue his jacket is, and his boots are yellow'. I can understand why Jackson left this part out – Tom Bombadil makes no further appearances in the story, and this episode doesn't seem to contribute anything to the wider plot. But Bombadil is one of the most compelling and extraordinary characters in the whole epic. He's a total one-off, living apart from all the great events affecting Middle Earth, completely secure against the rising evil of Sauron, but touching the action at one vital point, near the beginning – setting Frodo on his feet, in the right direction, and with real hope that the terrible power of Mordor is not the last word.

He's exactly like Melchizedek, who appears in the Old Testament in only two places: in Genesis 14:17–20, the story to which Hebrews refers in this section, and in Psalm 110:4, the verse already quoted in 5:6 and 6:20. The story in Genesis is every bit as odd as the Tom Bombadil episode in *The Lord of the Rings*. Abraham has just rescued his nephew Lot, and is coming home laden with plunder recaptured from the enemies who had seized Sodom, where Lot lived. He is met by 'Melchizedek king of Salem', who is also called 'priest of God Most High'. Melchizedek gives Abraham bread and wine, and blesses him in the name of 'God Most High'. Next Abraham gives Melchizedek a tenth (a tithe) of all the plunder. Then Abraham refuses to keep any more of the plunder, but gives it all back to the king of Sodom, saying that he has sworn to do so by 'the LORD, God Most High, Creator of heaven and earth', lest it should be said that Sodom had made Abraham rich.

That's it – apart from the mention in Psalm 110. How mysterious! Here's another complete one-off, just appearing in the story, recognized by Abraham as a priest of 'the LORD', the God he worships, albeit under a different name, so that Abraham is willing to be blessed by him, and gives him a tithe of the battle spoils.

We'll see in the next section exactly why Hebrews is so attracted to Melchizedek. Here we get the bones of his treatment.

First, his name (1–2). It means 'king of righteousness' in Hebrew, as the author points out. 'Righteousness' is a great Old Testament theme, a quality of God himself celebrated in many of the psalms. He is also 'king of Salem', that is, of Jerusalem, and the author rightly indicates that this means 'king of peace'. Peace is also a great Old Testament theme. It is the quality and experience of living in harmony with God and his world, under his blessing. It is often associated with 'righteousness'; see, for instance, the wonderful celebration of both in Psalm 85.

Secondly, his ancestry (3). He doesn't have any! He just appears, as if from nowhere. Of course, the author doesn't literally believe that the Melchizedek Abraham met had no parents. Nor does he literally believe that Melchizedek lived for ever (3, 8). He's concerned with how Melchizedek is presented in the Bible, in both Genesis 14 and Psalm 110. 'Parentage' is everything in biblical theology. 'Whose child are you?' – this question is essential to your whole identity in biblical thinking. Remember how Hebrews begins: 'In the past God spoke to our forefathers ...' (1:1). Our 'forefathers' are the first characters mentioned, after God. In the very next verses, we're going to hear about Levi and the significance attached to Levi's descent from Abraham. But Melchizedek? He belongs to no dynasty, to give him status. He's just *there*, a great intervention into the biblical story, blessing Abraham, 'like the Son of God'. It's almost as though he neither is born nor dies. And Abraham recognizes, simply by instinct, who he is.

Thirdly, his greatness (4–10). For the author, it's obvious that Melchizedek is 'greater' than Abraham, (a) because he 'blessed' Abraham, and (b) because Abraham gave him a tithe. These two things – blessing and tithes – come together, as the author reflects on the significance of tithes later on. The tribe of Levi was set apart to be priests on behalf of the rest of Israel, and they were supported by a tithe of the produce of the land. The Levites had no land of their own, because of their devotion to the priesthood. The other tribes sustained them, because the Levites mediated God's blessing to Israel. So both things, blessing moving in one direction, and the tithe moving in the other, indicate Abraham's submission to Melchizedek. Melchizedek must be greater than the Levites if he was greater than Abraham – this is the author's final comment (9–10).

What does 'greater' mean here (7)? More significant before God, more worthy of our attention, more powerful in mediating God's blessing. The end effect of verses 1–10 is: 'Here's someone you neglect at your peril!' The Hebrews had probably given Melchizedek no thought at all, hitherto – a character on the edges of biblical history, easily ignored. The thought that he might be greater than Abraham is truly challenging!

Questions

1. Here's a strange character, right outside the biblical covenants, but clearly on intimate terms with God. Can there be other such people? Tucked away in pagan cultures, unknown and ignored?
2. Melchizedek is the 'king of peace'. He lives in complete harmony with God, and his world – and yet he's surrounded by war in Genesis 14. How can we live out biblical peace, in a world of conflict? Is it possible? How?
3. These days Jerusalem, 'the city of peace', is particularly ill-named. What would Melchizedek, 'king of Salem', say to those involved in the terrible conflict around his city today? What would his counsel be?

7:11–22

Why Melchizedek?

Now we begin to discover how Melchizedek fits into Hebrews' argument. The point is – Jesus matches him, rather than Aaron.

We need to bear in mind why the author has introduced Melchizedek into his argument. It all started in 6:13–20, with the need to show how Jesus is the fulfilment of the promises to Abraham. So now we discover that Abraham's own 'priest' was not Aaron (his own descendant), but Melchizedek. Melchizedek appears, 'blessing' Abraham in parallel with God's own promise to him (6:13–14). And we discover that Psalm 110 proclaims this Melchizedek priesthood as 'for ever'. It wasn't just a one-off, at the time of Abraham. Remember that Psalm 110 was already applied to the Messiah, and to Jesus, by the first Christians – see Hebrews 1:13, and the comment there. So, if he can show that, scripturally, Jesus fulfils the requirements for this Melchizedek priesthood, the author will have achieved his purpose. Here is the one who can legitimately pronounce God's 'blessing' over the house of Abraham. It's beautifully tidy that God's oath to bless Abraham in Genesis 22 (6:13) is matched by God's oath to appoint the Melchizedek priest for ever in Psalm 110 (7:20–21).

In this central part of chapter 7 we hear the author's central arguments. The long verse 11 starts it off, by expressing the absolutely basic point. Why is Melchizedek there at all in the Old Testament? Once again, the author is looking for, and exploiting, tensions and contradictions. On the one hand, it looked as though the *Aaronic* priesthood was the thing – appointed by God in fulfilment of his promise to Abraham. On the other, however, the Old Testament contains another priesthood altogether, apparently even more significant. For Hebrews, the very presence of Melchizedek in the Old Testament undermines the reality and effectiveness of the 'levitical' or Aaronic priesthood. The Old Testament questions itself – and out of the tension emerges the need for Jesus, who resolves it, and thus allows the Old Testament to continue as God's word of truth. We'll see more of this as we go along.

Verses 12–19 then develop an argument out of the basic verse 11, and in support of it.

First, *an argument from within the law* (12–14). The law of Moses does not allow that any apart from the Levites can serve as priests. But Jesus was of the tribe of Judah! However, this does not disqualify him from priesthood, because the Melchizedek priesthood is associated with *King David* in Psalm 110. (We'll see a bit more about this in the 'Digging deeper' section that follows.) If Jesus represents a whole new kind of priesthood, then he will have a radical effect on the law, because the priests were the lawgivers. In fact, the whole law revolved around the 'cult', the organization of sacrificial practices, so if the cult is replaced by a new priesthood, the law will have to change as well.

Secondly, *an argument from Jesus' life* (15–17) – specifically, an argument from his resurrection. Jesus has shown us 'indestructible life' in his resurrection (16). The power of death could not hold him. Isn't this precisely what Psalm 110:4 requires of the Melchizedek priest? That priesthood is 'for ever' – it is not to be inherited from a predecessor, when the earlier postholder dies. Actually, Jews had such different views of the Messiah that not all Jews believed that the Messiah would live for ever. But many did – see John 12:34, where 'the crowd' says to Jesus, 'We have heard from the Law that the Christ [= Messiah] will remain for ever.' In fact, Psalm 110:4 may well be one of the verses in 'the Law' that are in mind here. And now we have Jesus, the Son of God, risen from the dead: who could fail to make the connection with Psalm 110? But if he *is* the Melchizedek priest, then things are going to change.

Thirdly, *a radical conclusion about how we must now 'approach' God* (18–19). The result of all this is that 'the former regulation is set aside because it was weak and useless' (18), and 'a better hope is introduced, by which we draw near to God' (19). This is so radical! Do the readers cotton on to what Hebrews is saying? Their whole beloved way of 'approaching' God, based on Old Testament law, is being set aside as 'weak and useless', and replaced by 'a better hope' given by Jesus. 'The law made nothing perfect,' comments the author drily (19). It simply didn't work – and this is the point he's going to develop at length in chapter 9. He just drops it in here, in passing. The chief point here is that the Melchizedek priesthood bypasses the Law and its regulations about cult and worship, and therefore requires a whole new way of 'approaching' God. The implication is clear: we need to listen to the Son of God, to hear from him how to worship God truly.

For he has now become 'the guarantee of a better covenant' (22). This is the first appearance of the word 'covenant' in Hebrews – a vital word that appears seventeen times altogether, and will be the crucial theme in chapters 8 – 10. It's a word that goes right back to Abraham. God's 'covenant' with him was the promise to be God to him and to his descendants for ever (Genesis 17:7). Now we've discovered that the Abrahamic covenant lands upon Jesus as its fulfilment, because he picks up the Melchizedek priesthood, which meant so much to Abraham at that one crucial moment in his life. What Abraham experienced just once, as he returned exhausted from the battle to save Lot and received Melchizedek's blessing, we experience again and again in our lives, as Jesus the Son of God pours out his blessing upon us, from day to day. A better covenant, indeed!

Questions

1. This argument is based not just upon biblical learning but also upon great theological creativity. Hebrews handles these biblical texts not just with skill but with novelty. What conclusions do you think we should draw from this when it comes to training teachers and leaders for the church today?
2. Do you think it's right to look for, or find, contradictions in the Bible? How should we handle it if we think we have found one? Can you think of examples?
3. In what ways is it 'better' to approach God through Jesus than through Old Testament religion, or through other religions known to you in the world today? What makes the experience of Jesus 'better'? Make a list – and then perhaps turn it into prayer.
4. Read the whole of Psalm 110. Can you see how the whole psalm fits into the author's beliefs about Jesus, and his presentation of him here?

Digging deeper: A bit more on Melchizedek

Melchizedek's arrival on the stage in Hebrews is so extraordinary that it's worth pausing and asking a bit more about this interesting character. Where did he come from? Does he make an appearance in other writings around the same time as Hebrews, or only here? And most important, is this argument around Melchizedek and his relation to Jesus completely potty, or can we see how it really makes sense? This last question may seem a bit irreverent towards Hebrews, but others have roundly accused the author of twisting Scripture for his own purposes, so we need to ask it.

Hebrews is not the only writing to feature Melchizedek around this time. Most especially, one of the Dead Sea

Scrolls is a 'Melchizedek' text. We don't know exactly when it was written, but certainly before AD 70 (which is probably also the cut-off date for Hebrews). It links Melchizedek with the messianic prophecy in Isaiah 61:1–2, and obviously sees Melchizedek as a kind of angelic deliverer, due to come in the last days to save Israel. The Jewish philosopher Philo was also writing about this time; he turns Melchizedek into an allegory of the Mind, which can pursue heavenly thoughts. About this time, too, a Melchizedek legend arose in which Melchizedek was miraculously born and miraculously preserved through Noah's flood, and then gave rise to a whole succession of priests, the last of which will appear at the end, a high priest called 'the word and power of God'. By contrast, the Jewish historian Josephus – a little bit later – just treats him as a historical figure, the priest-king of Salem.

Which all means simply that, while people were interested in Melchizedek, no-one really knew what to make of him.

Who was he, really? We can connect this question with the important one above, about whether Hebrews' treatment of him really makes sense, or is just as legendary and fantastic as some of the other treatments around. Many years ago the Old Testament scholar Aubrey Johnson suggested a line of historical connection that makes a lot of sense and gives Hebrews' use of Melchizedek real meat and substance:

▶ He notes first that Melchizedek was a 'priest-king' in Jerusalem – an unusual combination of these two roles, which were often kept separate in the ancient world.

▶ Next he observes that, in Joshua 10:1, at the time of the conquest (when the tribes of Israel were entering the promised land), the king of Jerusalem is called Adonizedek, which means 'lord of righteousness', virtually the same as Melchizedek ('king of righteousness').

90

▶ Next he observes the strange tradition that King David and his sons occasionally exercised priestly functions in Jerusalem – apparently in contravention of the law, which limited priesthood to the Levites. We see this, for instance, in David's case in 2 Samuel 24:25 (the first sacrifices on the future site of the temple), and in Solomon's case at the dedication of the temple (1 Kings 8:62). In 1 Kings 9:25 we discover that Solomon specifically offered sacrifices three times a year (which would have been at the three great pilgrim festivals).

▶ This tradition carries on with Zechariah's vision of the combined priestly and royal rulership in Jerusalem (Zechariah 4:12–14; 6:12–13), and with the aspiration of the leaders at the time of the Maccabees (second century BC) to combine both roles.

▶ So when we look at Psalm 110, which is a Davidic psalm, it's certainly tempting to put it all together as follows. There existed in Jerusalem, before ever it became David's capital city in Israel, a tradition of a priest-king ruling the city. 'Melchizedek' or 'Adoni-zedek' may have been a kind of dynastic title for this priest-king. When David took over the city (2 Samuel 5:6–10) he adopted the local tradition, 'became' Melchizedek, and attached priestly functions to his kingship. This is reflected in Psalm 110, where the role is projected forward on to the great coming King who is David's 'Lord'. But it also carried on historically in the occasional priestly practices of the sons of David.

Against this background, Hebrews makes a lot of sense. It is not fanciful to connect Jesus to this tradition, granted that he is being identified as the Davidic Messiah. And there really is a tension in the Old Testament between these two sorts of priesthood. Numbers 18 makes it clear that only the Levites can serve as priests – after this was tested, with disastrous results, in Numbers 16 – 17. Yet we also have the Davidic kings functioning as priests, without question or opposition.

The connection that Hebrews makes between Melchizedek and the promises of 'blessing' to Abraham, and the way he links 'for ever' in Psalm 110:4 to Jesus' resurrection – these are wonderful, creative pieces of biblical theology, which we can surely affirm and accept.

Hebrews stretches us in making us wrestle with a passage like chapter 7. In fact, the whole letter does. It's not just a matter of reading the meaning off the surface of the text, like a combine harvester skimming across a field. We have to dig, and weigh what we find, and do our best to get into our author's mind, in sympathy with him and the situation he was facing with the 'Hebrews', that difficult crowd of Jewish Christians needing to be gently coaxed into a better view of Jesus.

7:23–28

Jesus our great high priest again

The author draws the threads of this section together with a final passionate portrayal of Jesus the great high priest, fully designed to meet our need.

These final verses of the chapter look back to the beginning of the section in 4:14 – 5:10. Many of the themes introduced there are picked up again here (Jesus' sinlessness; the 'weakness' of the other high priests, offering sacrifices for their own sins; Jesus' appointment; his 'passing into the heavens', etc.). This is a deliberate technique often used by Bible writers – it's called the inclusio technique, because it rounds a section off by 'including' the contents within brackets formed by collections of the main themes, beginning and ending it.

What a summary! The author contrasts Jesus' high priesthood with that of the other, Aaronic high priests. As the Melchizedek high priest he is quite different from them. The contrast has three parts to it.

First, a *contrast of number and permanence* (23–25). There were lots of Aaronic high priests, because they kept dying off and needed to be replaced. But there's only one Jesus, who lives for ever. There's real irony here – we think back to 2:14–15, and the way our 'champion' has come to free us from the greatest enemy of humankind: death and the fear of it. The old high priests were completely useless where it really mattered. They couldn't even save themselves from death, let alone those who depended on them. But Jesus is different. Verse 25 is one of the most wonderful in the whole letter. Nobody is excluded from the scope and effectiveness of his high-priestly ministry, 'because he always lives to intercede for them'.

As high priest, his permanent 'life' is not devoted to his own enjoyment. He never lays down his office. And high priests 'intercede', that is (as we saw), they represent the people before God. Jesus does this too, for us. The word 'intercede' could be translated 'encounter': he encounters God for us, representing before God – so that God can't escape the sight! – a humanity fully redeemed and fit to stand before him. That's the basic idea. It's not so much that he prays for us ('Lord, please help Marty with his exams today') – although I'm sure he does this, too. It's more that he represents permanently, before God, all the reasons why we should be completely saved too, just like him, and enter the Most Holy Place where he is our forerunner. If he prays specific prayers for us, then they will be for strength and faithfulness on the journey as we follow in his footsteps.

Secondly, a *contrast of quality* (26–27). What a contrast! I love the word 'fitting' in verse 26 – it's the same word as in 2:10. There it was something that was 'fitting' for God as creator to do. Here it's something 'fitting' for us, not to do, but to have. We have a high priest who exactly 'fits' our need. He has been fully one of us, implicated no-holds-barred in all the mess and murk of our human existence. But he passed through all the horribleness unscathed (though not unhurt – see 5:7), unsullied by the grime and grot we specialize in. He never gave in to hatred, lust, revenge or greed. He never ended up compromising with sin or colluding with the scheming. He is 'set apart from sinners' (26) – although not of course distant from sinners who want him as Saviour. And now he is 'exalted above the heavens', present to God himself as our representative.

And the other high priests? Well, they were just like us, really – no better. They had to repeat their sacrifices over and over again, because they kept sinning themselves, just like us. But for Jesus, once was enough, for his offering of himself.

Thirdly, a *contrast of authority* (28). In the long run, it's what counts with God that counts. The author so wants his readers to see this. Even if they lived miles away from Jerusalem, Jews still felt themselves to be dependent on the sacrifices offered in the temple there, and paid a 'temple tax' annually to support them. The author's 'Hebrews' were still part of this system, belonging to their synagogue, and doubtless contributing the temple tax like all the rest. And now they're thinking of slipping back into that, and belonging only there. But why support and depend on a system that doesn't count with God?

On the one hand, the law appointed the high priests, who are subject to all the aforementioned weaknesses (sin, death, etc.). On the other hand, God himself appointed his Son to the Melchizedek priesthood by swearing an oath that his priesthood will be permanent – Psalm 100:4. And this oath was uttered after the law was given, thus superseding it, giving God's latest word on the 'priesthood' issue. Surely there's no competition? Who would choose the former over the latter? The very last word says it all – 'made perfect' (this is the last word in the Greek – a single, great resounding word). Before God, this high priest, 'the

Son', is made perfect, that is, he fulfils his ministry perfectly, because he has been through a process that has united him with us and enabled him fully to represent God to humanity, and humanity to God, and as one of us he died our death and has returned 'behind the veil' into the very presence of God. Who would choose Aaron or his successors in preference to this high priest? This is the high priest endorsed by God himself – 'made perfect for ever'.

But the author does not know if his Hebrews will accept his reading of the Old Testament or not. He seriously wants – as we have seen – to show that the Old Testament requires us to believe that Jesus, the Son of God, is the fulfilment of God's purposes for Israel. Obviously, this is of special relevance and importance for the first readers, in their particular situation. But it's pretty vital for us, too. For us, too, Jesus is the focus of God's provision. We lose him at our peril, and keep him to our eternal profit.

Questions

1. If you were threatened with persecution (unemployment, confiscation of property, imprisonment, ostracism by family, tarnishing of reputation, threats of physical injury to you or loved ones) for believing this message about Jesus, would you believe it, and say so publicly?
2. Look back over Hebrews 4:14 – 7:28. What are the things that have most struck you in this section? Where has God spoken to you most? Write down what you want to take away from this study most particularly. Share it with others in your group if possible.
3. What resolutions have you made, out of this study? What do you want to change about your life or relationships with God and with others? Remember the high priest who sympathizes with all our weaknesses.

JESUS' MINISTRY

Hebrews 8:1 – 10:39

Stop and look: What Jesus did

The argument of the letter so far has focused on who Jesus is. It's vital for the author's purposes that he convince his readers that Jesus is no minor Messiah. He's not just an extra prophet with extra powers to give, adding 'the powers of the coming age' (6:5) to all the blessings they already have as members of Israel and of the synagogue. He is so much more! He's the eternal Son, through whom the worlds were made, greater by far than all angels and prophets, and in his greatness uniquely sharing our flesh and blood. He steps into the weaknesses of the old covenant. Moses and Joshua never managed to bring Israel into 'the rest' of God. Aaron the high priest could not deliver people from the death to which he himself was subject. Jesus is a priest of a different order – the Melchizedek priest, fulfilling the promises to Abraham in an entirely different way.

But what does Jesus actually do, as high priest? Hebrews has argued his fitness for the office but, because it's a unique office, we don't know what his ministry will be. We've heard a few hints – as high priest he must have offered something (5:2), and his offering has been described as 'prayers and petitions with loud cries and tears' (5:7) and as simply 'himself' (7:27). But the author wants to communicate more than this, because he wants to show that only the ministry of Jesus is effective in bringing the forgiveness of sins and reconciliation between God and humankind.

So for the next three chapters (8–10) we focus on Jesus' ministry (what he did), as distinct from his office (who he is) – not that they can be separated, of course. But they can be considered separately.

Chapters 8 – 9 have a balanced structure. They begin and end by focusing on the place of Jesus' ministry (8:1–6; 9:23–28). In both cases, there is a contrast between his ministry and that of the 'earthly' priests. In between, there are three sections focusing on the theme of 'the covenant', again involving a contrast between old and new:

8:7–13   Old and new covenant in prophecy
9:1–14   Old and new covenant in the cult
9:15–22   Old- and new-covenant ratification

So 9:1–14 forms the heart of this section, and here verses 11–14 are the climax. In fact, those verses could claim to be the heart of the whole letter.

Then chapter 10 follows by applying the vision of the new covenant, in Jesus, to us. What does in mean, in practice, to believe that a new covenant has been 'ratified' – that is, set in place – by God through Christ? In different ways, this is the concern of the whole of chapter 10.

8:1–6

Greater ministry, better covenant, better promises

Where does the great high priest serve? In the heavenly sanctuary; the 'real' counterpart to the earthly one where the human priests offer sacrifices daily.

Chapter 8 verse 1 shows that we've got to a new point in the argument. 'The point of what we are saying is this ...' – or better, 'Now the whole point is ...' Following this, verses 1–2 say in a nutshell everything that the author will unpack over the next two chapters.

We do have such a high priest, he says. This is in response to 7:26, where he described the high priest who would fit our need. But do we have him, or are we just imagining an unreal ideal? No, we really have him! This high priest has sat down at God's right hand in heaven (see 1:3), where he is a servant in 'the sanctuary, the true tabernacle set up by the Lord, not by man'.

There's a lot to think about here. Whenever heaven, or the presence of God, is described in the Bible, temple symbolism is usually used to describe it. It wouldn't be putting it too strongly to say that, in the Bible, heaven is a temple. For instance, the book of Revelation repeatedly uses temple ideas – even temple furnishings – in describing the heavenly scene that appeared to John (see e.g. Revelation 8:3–5; 11:19; 15:5). This was partly because of the belief that God dwelt in the temple in Jerusalem, where of course he could not be contained, or confined – so the belief grew that the earthly temple was but a counterpart, or image, of the heavenly temple, which is much more fitted to contain him. Isaiah saw the two temples connected, in his great vision in Isaiah 6:1–7.

Paul develops the same idea in Galatians 4:24–26, where it's an earthly and a heavenly Jerusalem that match each other. And similarly in Revelation 21, John sees the heavenly Jerusalem coming down from heaven to earth, and then this great city is described as if it were a temple (Revelation 21:16, 22 – it has the dimensions of the sanctuary in the Old Testament temple, a perfect cube).

Where is all this leading? The author is arguing that Jesus is our high priest in the heavenly temple, where God really dwells – the temple where it really counts. This is the temple set up by the Lord, not by humankind. Paul does something similar in Galatians 4, where he argues that all believers in Jesus are citizens of the heavenly Jerusalem, not the earthly. Again, this is where citizenship really counts!

Our author develops this thought in verses 3–5, then draws a conclusion in verse 6. We can follow through the logic of his argument.

Verse 3: If Jesus really is the Melchizedek high priest, then he must have offerings to make. This stands to reason – making offerings is the essence of the high-priestly role.

Verse 4: But his offering must be different from the kind of offerings they make in the earthly temple, because there's no room for him there. There are no 'sits. vac.' adverts in the Jerusalem papers, looking for applicants for the priesthood there. The jobs are all taken, with priests scurrying around performing their legally prescribed duties round the clock.

Verse 5: They, of course, are serving a 'copy and shadow' of the real thing, the temple in heaven, which is where our high priest actually ministers. The author finds this indicated in Exodus 25:40, when Moses receives orders to build the tabernacle 'according to the pattern shown you on the mountain'. What attracts him about this verse is the word 'pattern', which matches his description of the earthly temple as a 'copy' and 'shadow' of the heavenly one. But none of his readers would dispute the reality of the heavenly temple, and the relation between the earthly and the heavenly – all Jews believed this. What his readers might have disputed is whether Jesus really has this final, conclusive high-priestly ministry in the heavenly temple, so that the ministry of the earthly temple is no longer needed. That's radical!

Verse 6: Our author doesn't state his conclusion quite as radically as that. That would be putting it a bit too bluntly for his readers. He wants to woo them into boosting their understanding of Jesus to better proportions. So he uses the language of comparison (Jesus is 'better'), and employs rather more theological language, stating it in a way that prepares his readers for what follows: 'the ministry Jesus has received is as superior to theirs as the covenant of which he is mediator is superior to the old one, and it is founded on better promises'.

But there's tragedy in the air, here, as we'll see in the 'Digging deeper' section after the next study (pp. 105–108). Verses 4–5 probably indicate that, at the time of writing, the Jerusalem temple was indeed still standing. But it can only have been a few years later when the whole thing was flattened by the Romans (AD 70), amid terrible suffering and trauma, and the sacrifices were never again restored. If the author lived to see this, he must have wished even more to be able make this argument powerful and convincing – for we depend before God, not on earthly sacrifices offered by an earthly priesthood, but on the heavenly ministry of a resurrected and glorified Melchizedek, sitting at God's right hand.

Questions

1. Do you think that there are still special 'places' on earth, 'sacred spaces' where God is specially present and which in some way match the heavenly temple where he lives? If so, what kind of places are they – and what role could or should they play in our lives?
2. 'He came to that which was his own, but his own did not receive him' (John 1:11). For various reasons, the leaders of first-century Judaism did not recognize Jesus as Messiah, and crucified him. Why does religion sometimes get things so terribly wrong? What warning do we need to hear?

8:7–13

Jeremiah and the new covenant

Here is scriptural proof for what he has just said. The author turns to Jeremiah and his famous 'new covenant' prophecy.

We've met some dramatic claims in 8:1–6. If the author is going to convince his 'Hebrews', he's going to need some powerful scriptural arguments. Nearly

all this section is taken up with a long quotation of Jeremiah 31:31–34 – the longest continuous Old Testament quotation in the New. And then, as with the quotation of Psalm 95 in chapter 3, and of Psalm 110 in chapter 5, the quotation forms the raw material for the following argument. The author is still chewing over Jeremiah 31 in chapter 10 – see 10:16–17.

Paul uses this passage, too, briefly, in 2 Corinthians 3:3–6, and also in Romans 2:15. But in both places he doesn't actually quote it; he just alludes to it, and he certainly doesn't rely on it as much as Hebrews does. For Hebrews, it's really a crucial passage. What does he find in it?

First, *he finds God himself questioning the continuance of the old covenant.* The author is following his usual technique, and exploiting places where the Old Testament seems to undermine itself. God himself seems to be responsible for this in Jeremiah. 'God' should probably be introduced into the translation of the opening comment in verse 7 – he's implied there: 'If the first covenant had been problem-free, God would not have made room for a second.' And then, within the quotation itself, God promises a new covenant not like the old one made under Moses at the exodus (9). God himself proclaims the end of the old covenant.

Secondly, *he finds a clear statement of the ineffectiveness of the old covenant.* The author signals this, too, in his introduction to the quotation: 'God found fault with the people and said …' (8). And then the quotation follows on, vividly: 'they did not remain faithful to my covenant, and I turned away from them, declares the Lord' (9). The basic relationship, which the covenant was meant to secure, was shattered. The author has written about all this in chapters 3 – 4. The exodus generation did not believe (4:2), and so God 'turned away' from them, and swore that they would not enter his 'rest', that intimate sharing of his life that had been the whole purpose of the exodus. Jeremiah was writing at a similarly terrible, tragic time, when the relationship between Israel and her God had been severed. The Babylonians had invaded and taken over the land, the temple had been destroyed, and thousands had been killed or carried away into exile. The old covenant just hadn't worked. So the time was ripe for a new one.

Thirdly, *he finds a wonderful promise of a new covenant*. God promises a whole new relationship with his people. That's what the word 'covenant' means, in fact. It's a legal term, denoting the regulation of the relationship between the consenting parties. The new covenant still keeps, at its heart, the basic promise to Abraham, 'I will be God to you and to your descendants' (Genesis 17:7) – Jeremiah picks this up in verse 10: 'I will ... be your God and the God of your descendants after you.' But around this commitment the relationship is completely recast, to make sure that it works this time. There is to be:

▶ *A new place for the law* (10). Instead of being written on stone tablets, the law is going to have new receptacles – the minds and hearts of the people. So their response to their Lord – their obedience – will be from the heart. This links to the next new thing:

▶ *A new knowledge of God* (11). Previously, it had to be 'taught' (especially by the priests). But now the knowledge of God will be instinctive, and will transcend status and education ('from the least of them to the greatest').

▶ *A new forgiveness of sins* (12). This is actually the foundation of everything – note the 'For' at the beginning of verse 12 (which should be stronger, really: '*Because* I will forgive their wickedness ...'). In Jeremiah's day this was vital. The events leading up to the exile called for massive forgiveness. But God promises it! And our author is delighted to record it. God *wants* to stay in relationship with his people, on new terms.

The conclusion in verse 13 is the author's only direct comment on his quotation from Jeremiah, although the quotation lurks in the background throughout chapter 9. 'By calling this covenant "new", he has made the first one obsolete; and what is obsolete and ageing will soon disappear.' From the author's perspective, the old covenant is past its sell-by date. You can buy it if you want, but it won't do you much good. And he thinks this is clearly taught in Jeremiah 31. In the two chapters that follow, he tries to work this out as he looks in detail at the working of the covenants, old and new, in contrast with each other.

Questions

1. What do you think it means to have God's law written on your heart? Do you feel this is true for you? Have a look at 2 Corinthians 3:3–6 for Paul's understanding of it.
2. 'They shall not teach one another' (11, NRSV). But surely we need teachers in the church? This is one of the spiritual gifts in 1 Corinthians 12:28 and Ephesians 4:11. What do Jeremiah and the author of Hebrews mean here?
3. How would we begin to explain the message of Hebrews to Jewish friends and neighbours? (There's a 'Digging deeper' section on this below, but why not think about it and discuss it first before reading it?)

Digging deeper:
Hebrews and the Jewish people

Many Jewish people have found Hebrews deeply offensive. This is hardly strange. The author proclaims their covenant obsolete and ineffectual, and argues very passionately that these Jewish Christians should give up their trust in the Abrahamic covenant and believe only in Jesus. He attacks Moses, arguing that Jesus is far greater, that Moses was a failed leader, that the cult instituted in the law of Moses is ineffective, and that God intends something much 'better'. Not surprisingly, some Jews have accused Hebrews of being anti-Semitic. How would you respond to this charge?

We can't ignore this question, because these days relationships between the religions are discussed much more openly, and the whole issue of Christian anti-Semitism is a truly hot potato. I'm afraid that there's a long and very sad history involved here. Yes, in the history of the church some Christians have taken very hostile attitudes towards Jews and encouraged violence towards them; and yes, the theology of Hebrews has been appealed to as justification for such attitudes and actions. You can see how this would work: in a situation where there's a strong sense of division between Christian and Jewish communities, Hebrews provides ammunition for Christians to say that the Jews have misunderstood their own Scriptures and are deliberately clinging to a way of life that God has declared obsolete – living in deliberate disobedience. At times and in places where church and state were closely linked, it was not difficult for Christian persecution of Jews to result – especially since, at the back of it all, lay the accusation that the Jews had crucified the Son of God.

How should we respond to this? I've got three points to make here.

First, *anti-Semitism is hatred of Jews, and this is never commended in the New Testament* – certainly not in Hebrews. This author loves his readers, looks forward to being with them (13:23), asks them to pray for him (13:18), and lets his concern for them ooze from every word of the letter. He's written a masterpiece, for them only – a work that must have taken tremendous effort and time. Whether they were convinced or not, they could not accuse him of failing to love them. Sadly, however, Jews can certainly accuse Christians of such failure, at many times and in many places.

Secondly, *Hebrews was written within Judaism*. Yes, it's a Jewish work. I've put this deliberately in a provocative way. Your reaction might well be, 'No, it's not Jewish, it's essentially Christian: isn't that why it's in the New

Testament? It focuses on Jesus.' Your reaction arises from our situation today, where 'Christianity' and 'Judaism' are two distinct religions, and have been so for centuries. But at the time of the writing of Hebrews, the parting of the ways between the two communities was by no means complete. And for the first readers of this letter, it hadn't begun. At least, they were just beginning to feel the pressure to choose one rather than the other (see the 'Digging deeper' section on their situation, above, pages 32–35).

Within the first three to four decades after Pentecost, there were

1. Christian Jews still living fully as part of the Jewish community. Among New Testament writers, James represents this group. And of course this is where the first readers of Hebrews are.

2. Christian Jews still fully Jewish in allegiance, but deeply re-evaluating their Judaism because of their experience of Jesus, and possibly forced to separate themselves from the Jewish community because of persecution. Among New Testament writings, Hebrews, the Gospel of John and the book of Revelation illustrate this group.

3. Christian Jews who had virtually moved right outside Jewish circles, and were living as Gentiles in Gentile fellowships, supporting Gentile missions (but still longing for the conversion of Israel). Within the New Testament, Paul and Luke exemplify this.

4. Gentile Christians who were aware of the Jewish roots of their new faith and received the Old Testament Scriptures as 'Christian', but who lived outside Judaism and felt no need for particular contact with Jewish communities. Among New Testament writers, this group is not represented at all.

What differences! The church today, of course, is almost 100% situated in group 4, and this has been the case since very soon after New Testament times – even though none of the New Testament authors fall into this category. But because Hebrews was written by a Jew, within Judaism (which included Christian Judaism), and for Jews, it's possible for the author to say things that will sound very different if they are said by Gentiles in support of a programme to criticize or even vilify Jews. The author must have argued these points through with Jews, as well as with Christian Jews – and in that first-century setting no-one would accuse him of anti-Semitism or regard him as less than fully Jewish. It's so important to get our history right!

Thirdly, *the author is really very gentle in the way he communicates his 'better' view of Jesus.* He's very subtle. He could blast them out of the water, telling them they're outmoded and old-fashioned, that their theology is grotty, and that they ought to be like him, moving with the times. But no – he takes them seriously, expressing his deep concern for them, of course, but taking the time and trouble to argue the whole issue through, and to do it in a way that could gently persuade them that he is right. For instance, he never actually mentions the temple in Jerusalem – the word 'temple' never occurs in Hebrews, even though its rituals and religion are so central to his concern. He constructs his argument around the 'tabernacle', the movable sanctuary that was the predecessor to the temple. He leaves his readers to make the logical connection to the contemporary equivalent. Also, he never tells them to leave the synagogue and stop worshipping with their fellow Jews. He just doesn't want them to give up worshipping Jesus!

We need to have the same attitude, I suggest, in all our relationships with Jewish people. Of course, we can't stop believing what we believe. But there needs to be a gentleness, respect and love that might begin to make up for the centuries of hostility. And only so shall we truly be faithful followers of Jesus the Jew.

'Purifying the conscience'

The author shows how the prophecy of a new covenant makes sense when we actually look at the old-covenant provisions for the forgiveness of sins and for fellowship with God.

At first sight this is one of the most difficult parts of Hebrews to understand, but appearances are deceptive. The first readers would not have found it at all difficult – the problem arises just from our lack of familiarity with Old Testament religion.

The author describes the 'tabernacle', the portable sanctuary that the Israelites took with them on their journey to the promised land. Its construction is described in Exodus 25 – 31 and 35 – 40. There are many details about the construction and furnishings in Exodus, and the author comments that he'd like to go into them all (5). But that would have diverted him from his main point, because there is just one aspect of the tabernacle that he wants to emphasize – its division into two halves.

He calls them two 'tents', the first (2, 6), and the second (3–5, 7). The temple was constructed with the same division, so the plan of the temple on page 119 will help here. The first 'tent' was the outer part of the tabernacle, called 'the Holy Place' (2). The second 'tent' was the inner sanctuary, where 'the ark of the covenant' was kept, and this was called 'the Most Holy Place' (3). The author mentions that the cherubim were in the second tent – these, with the closely related seraphim, were angelic winged creatures, thought to inhabit the heavenly temple (see e.g. Psalm 80:1; Isaiah 6:2). There were two wooden cherubim in the tabernacle (in the temple they were overlaid with gold). God says to Moses in Exodus 25:22, 'There, above the cover between the two cherubim that are over the ark of the Testimony, I will meet with you and give you all my commands for the Israelites.' So the tabernacle was the point of encounter between God and his people, and thus also the point of revelation. The inner sanctuary (the second tent) represented that crossover zone, the place where this world intersects with the world of God's glory and holiness. In his vision in the temple in Isaiah 6:1–8, Isaiah sees the seraphim flying around – not the gold representations in the earthly temple (Exodus 25:18–20) but the real ones that inhabit the heavenly temple.

So the inner sanctuary, the Most Holy Place, was a danger zone. God's presence is always a threat in the Old Testament: sinners, beware! The paradox is that the very place that was meant to be the point of meeting was actually a symbol of separation. Only the high priest was allowed into the Most Holy Place, just once a year, on the Day of Atonement, making sure that he was protected by sacrificial blood, 'which he offered for himself and for the sins the people had committed in ignorance' (7). In fact the regular name for the tabernacle was 'the tent of meeting' (e.g. Leviticus 16:33), which is precisely what it was not.

The author claims a special revelation from the Holy Spirit about the meaning of this strange paradox: that 'the way into the sanctuary [i.e. the heavenly temple, the real place of God's presence] has not yet been disclosed, as long as the first tabernacle still stands' (8, my translation). Here 'first tabernacle' has two meanings. At its basic level, it means that the outer section barred the way, and stopped access to the inner sanctuary. But its second, more significant, meaning is that, so long as the old tabernacle/temple system of worship remains in force, there will never be access into the presence of God for the likes of you and me. God remains separate, isolated in holy loneliness.

The result, in verses 9–10, is that, under the old covenant, there can be perfected worship, but not perfected worshippers. All the rituals can be in place, but they are just 'regulations of the flesh' (10, NIV has 'external regulations'). What we really need, however, is to be 'perfected in conscience' (9; NIV has 'clear the conscience'), and this cannot be delivered by ceremonial actions alone. 'Perfecting in conscience' is what Jeremiah is talking about when he looks forward to the writing of the law on the heart (8:10). All these rituals were just looking forward to 'the time of the new order' (10), or 'the time to set things right' (NRSV) – which is precisely what Jeremiah foresaw. There needs to be a new and better way that really opens up communication between us and God and enables us truly to 'enter his rest'.

Which is what Christ has done! Verses 11–12: for the first time, the author specifies exactly what Jesus offers. It's his own blood, which he takes with him into the heavenly sanctuary, 'the greater and more perfect tabernacle' where God truly dwells. This is new-covenant ministry. We remember Jesus' own words at the Last Supper: 'This cup is the new covenant in my blood' (Luke 22:20; 1 Corinthians 11:25): Hebrews just spells out the theology of this. The author explains how this new-covenant sacrifice differs so radically from the old.

Verses 13–14 are a wonderful summary of the theology of Hebrews. All that old-covenant stuff is OK, as far as it goes – it gets you prepared. It 'cleanses the flesh' ready to enter the presence of God. But then it slams the door shut, and locks God away in the 'Most Holy Place'! We need more – a true 'cleansing of the conscience'. And it's the blood of Christ that does this, cleansing the part of us where the moral and spiritual power of sin is felt. He offered himself 'by the eternal Spirit' to God, because his sacrifice was a spiritual one, even though it involved his physical blood. He offered 'himself' in his humanity to the God to whom he was intimately related by the Spirit. And that sacrifice will 'cleanse' us, too, because we are 'of one' with him (2:11). He opens the shut door into the heavenly sanctuary and fits us to 'serve the living God'. Praise him!

There's more about this in the 'Digging deeper' section on the Day of Atonement below.

The author has more to say about this 'cleansing of the conscience' in chapter 10. Before we get there, however, he wants to continue his comparison of the old and new covenants.

Questions

1. Why do you think God set up a system of sacrifices and rituals that ultimately could not 'perfect the worshipper'? What was the point? Verse 9 may help with this.
2. Some churches still have a so-called 'sanctuary', an area meant to symbolize the special presence of God. In Orthodox churches it is very clearly separated from the rest of the church, symbolizing the distinction between heaven and earth. Is this a good thing? Or has the distinction between 'the sacred' and 'the secular' been completely broken down by Jesus?
3. It looks as though the author claims the revelation of the Holy Spirit for his comment about the relationship between the two 'tents' in verse 8. Do you think that the Holy Spirit still reveals scriptural interpretation in this way? How can we be sure that it's from him?

Digging deeper: The Day of Atonement and 'dead works'

The ritual of the Day of Atonement was one of the most dramatic in the religious calendar. It's described in Leviticus 16, the chapter to which the author alludes in his first reference to 'the veil' in 6:19. There were really three dramas, linked with each other. First the high priest had to sacrifice a bull for himself and his family, and a goat as a 'sin offering'. Then, he took the blood of the goat into the Most Holy Place, along with special incense, and sprinkled the blood inside, in order to 'make atonement for the sanctuary' (Leviticus 16:16, my translation). We'll think about this odd-sounding feature of the Day when we get to Hebrews 9:23–25. When the tabernacle and the first temple were standing, the ark of the covenant was in the Most Holy Place, but at the time of the writing of Hebrews the Most Holy Place in the temple was empty, with just a stone slab there.

Then the high priest emerged again, often to a rapturous reception. There's a wonderful description in the apocryphal book of Ecclesiasticus (or Ben Sirach) of the re-emergence of the high priest, like the sun rising. He'd made it! His acceptance by God – the fact that he came out alive – meant that God accepted the whole people. Then (the third dramatic action) the high priest recited the sins of Israel over the head of a second goat, which was driven away into the wilderness, symbolizing the banishing of their sins into the waste places outside the bounds of the covenant relationship with God. They can affect the relationship no more!

There's a particular feature of the Day of Atonement rituals, and theology, which seems to have meant a lot to the author of Hebrews – another of those points where he picks up a feature of Old Testament thinking that doesn't make sense and requires explanation provided now in Christ. Officially, the Day of Atonement was meant to 'hoover up' all the sins that had been left unatoned for over the previous twelve months – in particular, as Hebrews says, 'the sins the people had committed in ignorance' (9:7). If you were aware of a sin, then it would be possible to make atonement straight away. But one of the fears people had concerned the effect of unintentional sins: what if you committed a sin and weren't aware of it? The Day of Atonement was meant to cover all these, for the whole nation, for a whole year.

However, there was one category of sin for which no atonement could be made, not even on the Day of Atonement. This is called the 'high-handed' or 'defiant' sin, described in Numbers 15:30–31: 'anyone who sins defiantly, whether native-born or alien, blasphemes the

LORD, and that person must be cut off from his people. Because he has despised the LORD 's word and broken his commands, that person must surely be cut off; his guilt remains on him.' A 'high-handed' or 'defiant' sin was one which involved a deliberate rejection of the central demands of the covenant – an eyes-open 'blasphemy' of God's will and way. The only way of dealing with such sin was the death of the sinner.

But this leaves a real problem. There must be a grey area, between 'ordinary' sins, which can be covered by sacrifice, and 'defiant', 'high-handed' sins, which can't. Who decides which category sins fall into? The examples in Numbers are not exactly encouraging. We immediately hear of a man gathering sticks on the Sabbath. This is pretty flagrant 'work' – but is it a 'high-handed' sin? He is put under guard until the Lord reveals that it was 'high-handed', and the man is stoned to death (Numbers 15:32–36).

But the Lord doesn't give special instructions in every case of doubt, and there must have been many. And then we come to King David. With his eyes fully open, knowing exactly what he was doing, David committed adultery with the wife of Uriah the Hittite, and then had Uriah murdered so that he could marry her. If this is not 'defiant' sin, it would be hard to know what is! It sounds much worse than gathering sticks on the Sabbath.

But David is forgiven when he repents. There is no question of execution. Nathan the prophet simply says to him, 'The LORD has taken away your sin. You are not going to die' (2 Samuel 12:13). In Psalm 51, associated with this incident, David expresses his awareness that there could be no sacrifice to cover this sin (51:16). In this situation, 'the sacrifice acceptable to God is a broken spirit' (51:17, NRSV). But how is this possible, when the laws of the cult say that either sins must be atoned for by sacrifice or the sinner must die?

The tension is left unresolved within the Old Testament. But it is highly likely that, when he refers to being cleansed from 'dead works' in 9:14, the author of Hebrews has in mind precisely these sins of 'high-handed rebellion' against the Lord. 'Dead works', that is, works that should lead to our death, are covered by the death of Jesus, because he cleanses our conscience, that part of us that is truly sullied by rebellion of heart against God. The NIV is probably right to translate this expression as 'acts that lead to death', but they are acts that lead to death in this particular sense, that no sacrifice could atone for them – except, now, for the sacrifice of Christ.

This fits with the way 9:14 leads into 9:15, where the author makes it clear that the death of Jesus is retrospective in effect; it clears sins committed under the first covenant, so that old-covenant sinners like David might find salvation too.

The Day of Atonement thus reaches its fulfilment in Jesus. People could always hope that what they feared might be 'high-handed' sin would nevertheless be covered by the rituals of that day. If they didn't die, they concluded that it was! But it is actually the conscience-cleansing death of Christ that delivers us from the death deserved by our defiance against God.

9:15–28

'Purifying the sanctuary'

Three more ways in which the sacrifice of Jesus secures something better than sacrifices under the old covenant – three more reasons to trust and follow him.

As we saw in the outline on page 98–99 above, there are really two mini-sections here, which we take together. The first deals with how the covenant is inaugurated (9:15–22), and the second with how the sanctuary is purified (9:23–28). But actually we can divide it up a bit more satisfyingly than this, if we focus on the question: what does the blood of Jesus achieve? We can think of this as following on from the last section. There we just heard that his offering of himself cleanses our conscience (9:14). This was only a part of what Jeremiah prophesied – the last bit, basically the new forgiveness of sins (8:12). We need to know how this amounts to a whole new covenant – because in theory the forgiveness of sins could have been provided in a new way under the old covenant. A whole new recasting of the relationship with God? That's what the second half of chapter 9 sets out to show. What does the blood of Jesus achieve? Three glorious things.

First, *the inauguration of a new covenant* (15–22). The death of the Son of God must be something special. In fact, this was a question that the first Jewish Christians wrestled with. Why did the Messiah have to die? It seemed so inappropriate. See Peter's reaction to the thought in Matthew 16:21–23. Jewish Christians with an 'icing on the cake' Christology like our 'Hebrews' had no answer to this question. But die he did, and he himself put great emphasis on it, saying that he died as 'a ransom for many' (Mark 10:45). But as soon as people began to follow this thought up, and to say, 'He died as a sacrifice for sins', it called into question the effectiveness of the sacrifices for sins already available. We find Paul wrestling with this logic in Galatians 2:19–21 – look this up if you want to see Paul's train of thought on it.

The author of Hebrews is uncompromising. As great an event as the death of the Messiah must be matched by a purpose as great as the beginning of a whole new covenant – as Jeremiah prophesied. And our author backs this up with two thoughts about covenants, one practical and the other scriptural. His practical observation is that covenants, or wills (the same Greek word means both), always come into effect when someone dies (16–17). And his scriptural thought is that the first covenant was inaugurated by blood – a lot of 'sprinkling' recorded in Exodus

24:3–8 (18–21). So wouldn't we conclude that the death of the Messiah has the same effect?

Secondly, *the cleansing of the sanctuary* (23–26). This was actually a very important focus of the ritual of the Day of Atonement. In fact, the whole point of the high priest's visit into the Most Holy Place was to 'make atonement for the Most Holy Place' (Leviticus 16:16). The unintentional sins of the people were officially atoned for by the second goat – a ritual that took place after the high priest came out (and to which Hebrews does not refer). Why did the Most Holy Place, the sanctuary, need cleansing, as well as the people?

The best answer starts from the thought of the closeness of the tabernacle to the people. One writer has suggested that we need to distinguish between sin and impurity in understanding Leviticus. Sin attached to the people when they broke God's law. And impurity attached to the tabernacle when the people sinned. He describes impurity as a kind of mud that flew towards the holiness of the tabernacle, in the midst of the people, and stuck to it; and blood as the 'ritual detergent' that washed it off.

His language is vivid, but has truth in it. Because God is so close to his people, he needs to be protected from becoming contaminated by their sin. This is vividly symbolized by the 'cleansing of the sanctuary' on the Day of Atonement. But the author of Hebrews, of course, believes that all the elements of the Day of Atonement have their counterpart in reality, that is, in the real relationship between God and the world in Christ. So the blood of Jesus serves to cleanse the heavenly sanctuary, and this he has done by entering it on our behalf, bearing his own blood (23–24). He needs to do this only once, unlike the annual visit of Aaron and his sons, because his sacrifice is effective 'once for all' (25–26).

This prompts some interesting thoughts about where heaven is. Where would you locate it? Wherever it is, it must be close to us, if it needs to be 'cleansed' from contamination arising from proximity, like the old tabernacle.

Thirdly, *final salvation for the waiting crowds* (27–28). On the Day of Atonement, the high priest appeared out of the sanctuary to a rousing cheer from those waiting outside (see the 'Digging deeper' section on pages 119–122). The author applies this to the second coming of Jesus. We have to die and face judgment (27), but this is nothing to fear, because Jesus died and will come back to save us. The judgment of God is pronounced as the high priest reappears from the sanctuary – the sacrifice has been accepted once again. In just the same way, the judgment of God is pronounced as Jesus reappears 'to save those who are eagerly waiting for him' (28, NRSV). Whether already dead or still alive when he comes, we 'eagerly await' the re-appearance of our Saviour.

Questions

1. 'Without the shedding of blood there is no forgiveness' (9:22). Why is this? Why can't God just forgive us?
2. Where exactly is heaven? If someone put you on the spot with this question, what would you say? You might find it helpful to look at the book of Revelation in thinking about this, especially Revelation 1.
3. Contemporary Christians, at least in western churches, don't lay much emphasis on the second coming of Jesus. When did you last hear a sermon or teaching on it? Is this inevitable now that so much time has elapsed? What should we think and teach about it?
4. What's the most important thing about the parallels between the Day of Atonement and the sacrifice of Christ that you really want to hold on to and treasure? What has spoken most to you as you've studied Hebrews 9? Write it down, and share it with others.

Digging deeper: The design of the temple

Look at the plan of the temple in Jerusalem at the time of the writing of Hebrews. It's important to think about the design of the *temple* at the time of Hebrews, rather than the plan of the *tabernacle*. As we noted above, the author's real concern is with the theology of his readers and its effect on their attitude to Jesus. And their theology revolved around the significance of the temple, even though they may not have lived near it. In my view Hebrews was certainly written while the temple was still standing. If it had been destroyed before the letter was written, it's inconceivable that the author would have failed to mention such a terrible event. It would have actually fitted in with his message, dreadful though the tragedy was: he could have said, 'The old covenant is clearly drawing to an end.' So Hebrews was probably written around AD 65, just a short while before the destruction in AD 70.

We do not know where the readers lived. One of the options is Jerusalem, and this is certainly possible. In Jerusalem, more than anywhere else, we can imagine a complete group of Jewish Christians who can be addressed as a single community. This might be possible also in Rome, where there could have been a house church composed of Jewish Christians (see Romans 16). Hebrews 13:24 might make most sense if they are in Rome – 'Those from Italy send you their greetings.' Absent friends who have moved away from Italy are sending greetings back home.

But even if they lived in Rome the temple in Jerusalem will still have been very important for them. Notice the concentric structure – it's really a series of increasingly holy spaces contained within each other, like a Russian doll. First, outside the perimeter wall, there's the city of Jerusalem, the chosen, holy city, the heart of the 'holy land'. The whole land could be called 'God's sanctuary', for instance in Psalm 114:2. Then, within the wall, the first area is the big Court of the Gentiles, so called because Gentiles could enter it. The next court in was called the Court of the Women, because only Jews were allowed in, and women could go no further. By the gate into this court was a notice which said, 'Men of another race who enter here have only themselves to blame when their death follows.' Paul was accused of bringing Gentiles through this gate (Acts 21:28). The issue was purity. The 'holy place' at the centre of the temple must be protected from defilement. The further you go in, the greater the level of holiness.

The next court was the Court of Israel, where male Jews could enter. Then the Court of the Priests, the small courtyard outside the sanctuary itself, where the main altar stood and the sacrifices were offered daily. By rote, priests were also allowed to enter the outer part of the sanctuary, which stood at the very heart of the whole temple complex, to offer incense on the altar that stood before the Most Holy Place. There were so many priests that each could expect to do it only once in his lifetime. That's what Zechariah was doing when the angel told him that Elizabeth would give birth to a son, John the Baptist (Luke 1:8–23).

Finally, right at the centre, behind a tall and very thick curtain or 'veil', lay the Most Holy Place, known literally as 'the Holy of Holies' because it was the epicentre of holiness in the entire 'holy land'. Here only the high priest went, once a year on the Day of Atonement. Here, supremely, God was thought to be present, living in the centre of his people, but in splendid isolation because of his own holiness. The veil in front of the Holy of Holies was torn in two when Jesus died (Mark 15:38).

The temple generated huge loyalty and affection. Jews would travel from all over the Mediterranean world to attend festivals there. It truly was the place 'where all the Jews come together' (John 18:20). Because of the temple tax, paid by all Jews all over the world, the temple became

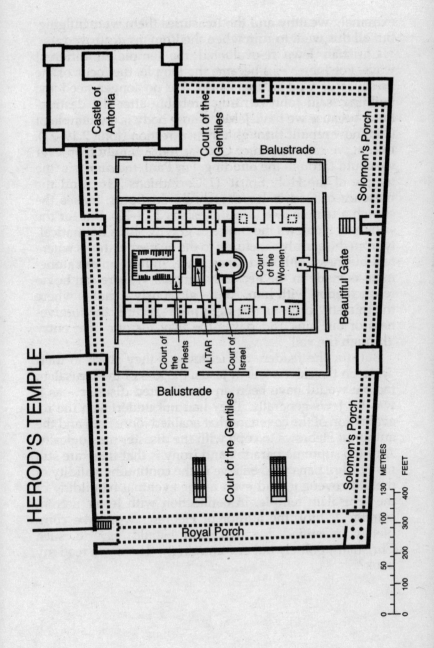

HEROD'S TEMPLE

Castle of Antonia

Court of the Gentiles

Balustrade

Solomon's Porch

Court of the Priests

ALTAR

Court of Israel

Court of the Women

Beautiful Gate

Balustrade

Court of the Gentiles

Solomon's Porch

Royal Porch

FEET   400   300   200   100   0
METRES 130   100   50   0

extremely wealthy and the treasuries there were bulging. But all this went to ruin when the Romans destroyed it.

Christian Jews re-evaluated the temple in different ways. For John, *Jesus* became the temple, the focus of the presence of God in the world. We no longer need the building, said John (writing probably after the destruction), because we have Jesus, whose body is the temple of God, now rebuilt through the resurrection (John 2:19–21). In him we can encounter God far more closely than ever we could through the building. For Paul, the *church* is 'the temple of the Holy Spirit' (1 Corinthians 3:16), and the presence of God in his church, by the Spirit, makes the church a temple (see also Ephesians 2:19–22). But for the author of Hebrews the centre of gravity shifts dramatically from the earthly sanctuary to the heavenly: this is where real business with God takes place. In fact, unless atonement is made in the heavenly sanctuary, there can be no reconciliation with him. And – gloriously – that is where the ministry of Jesus our high priest secures the forgiveness of our sins and paves the way for our own entry 'through the veil'.

But, for the readers of Hebrews, if they stuck to their 'icing on the cake' view of Jesus, the loss of the Jerusalem temple would have been an unmitigated disaster – as it was for Jews generally. They had not undertaken the re-evaluation of the covenant that enabled John, Paul and the author of Hebrews to cope with the disaster theologically. And the supreme paradox and irony is that there are still many Christians who believe in the continuing validity of the old covenant, and even in the eventual rebuilding of the Jerusalem temple, in connection with Jesus' second coming. I think the author of Hebrews would be completely mystified by this, and would say to such Christians, politely but encouragingly, 'Have you read my book?'

Perfected for all time

We come back to the contrast with which this section began in 8:1–6, and see how different Jesus' sacrifice is, and how effective, and how much desired by God.

Hebrews is so beautifully structured. Different patterns of thought often interweave with each other, so that it's possible to analyse passages in several ways. Here, even though the translations are probably right to put a paragraph division at 10:1, there's a beautiful pattern that crosses it:

A   9:26–28   Jesus' once-for-all, effective sacrifice for us.
  B   10:1–4   In contrast: the repeated, ineffective
    sacrifices of the old covenant.
    C   10:5–6   God didn't really want those
      sacrifices, anyway.
      D   10:7   He wanted a much fuller
        obedience to his will.
    C'   10:8   So, in place of the sacrifices he didn't
      want ...
      D'   10:9–10   Jesus offers himself, and
        does God's will by saving us.
  B'   10:11   So instead of the repeated, ineffective
    sacrifices in the temple ...
A'   10:12–14   Jesus' single sacrifice is effective for ever.

It's another 'in-out' pattern, with the central bit (CD) repeating itself in parallel for emphasis. It shows us that the author is beginning to draw conclusions at the end of the section that began in 8:1. And this pattern also helps us to see, not only the author's train of thought, but also the crucial focus of his thinking. This is that Jesus does the will of God by offering himself for us. It's vital to see from the outset that the phrase 'by that will' in verse 10 refers to the will of God (the NRSV helpfully translates it 'by God's will').

This is so important. Some ways of describing the atonement almost drive a wedge between God and Jesus. They say: God the Father is a God of supreme justice, and his justice requires that sin be punished. Blood must be shed. God the Son sheds his blood on our behalf, bears the necessary punishment for sin, and thus provides what the Father's justice demands, in order to forgive us. So the problem is God's, not ours (he can't forgive sin without a death), and the Son is on our side, achieving forgiveness by giving God what he needs.

There's a 'Digging deeper' section on pages 132–135, to explore it a bit further. But for now we just note that this is not what Hebrews says. The Son of God is not working to wrest forgiveness from the arms of a reluctant and angry Father. He comes to do God's will in a more perfect way than anyone had ever done it, even by perfect obedience to the law. He and the Father are absolutely one – remember 1:3, 'the outshining of his glory and the perfect imprint of his nature' (my translation)? There is no competition between them in atonement, to see whether the Father's justice or the Son's compassion will prove stronger.

The details of this passage are so powerful. Let's look at them briefly.

The Day of Atonement ritual, by its very repetition, reveals its inadequacy (1–4). If it worked, wouldn't people feel no need to repeat it, if they really felt saved from their sins? The whole point was that it *didn't* save them. It just patched things up, after the event, at the end of each year. In this, it was merely 'a shadow of the good things that are coming' (1), a massive visual aid helping us to understand the real thing, the once-for-all atonement of Jesus.

In any case, the Old Testament itself reveals that God

didn't really want the sacrifices (5–8)! Here, again, our author is working with a contradiction within the Old Testament, not in order to discredit it, but in order to show how necessary Jesus is to complete it and to help us to understand it as God's true word. On the one hand, it's clear that God 'commanded' the sacrificial system – in fact, this is the word used in Exodus 24:8, the verse quoted in Hebrews 9:20: 'This is the blood of the covenant, which God has commanded you to keep.' But on the other hand, Psalm 40:6 says clearly that 'sacrifice and offering you did not desire ... burnt offerings and sin offerings you did not require'. How do we square this circle? The answer is (a) to allow Psalm 40 – another royal psalm, ascribed to David – to point forward to Jesus, and (b) then to reread the Old Testament sacrificial system as a shadow, preparing the way for the greater 'doing of the will of God' towards which the psalm points.

This is really the issue we looked at above, in the 'Digging deeper' section on the Day of Atonement (pages 112–115), concerning the 'acts that lead to death' of 9:14. Within the Old Testament itself, there's a prophetic awareness of a level of forgiveness, given by God to his people, which cannot be accounted for within the cult. We looked at the instance of David's forgiveness for his sins against Uriah, but on a bigger scale there's the whole return from exile. How are the terrible sins that led to Israel's exile to Babylon atoned for? There's no answer – except that the Lord presents himself as Israel's redeemer. 'Do not fear, you worm Jacob, you insect Israel! I will help you, says the LORD; your Redeemer is the Holy One of Israel' (Isaiah 41:14, NRSV). For the author of Hebrews, we now see how this was possible, and what the Lord has done to redeem his people, quite apart from the 'cult'.

This section finishes with a glorious reminder of Psalm 110 in verses 12–13 – to underline (a) the *completeness* of Jesus' work (he has sat down), and (b) its *incompleteness* (his enemies are not yet finally conquered). There's a paradox here, to which the author returns in chapter 12.

Questions

1. We *have been* sanctified (10); he *has* perfected us 'for ever' (14); we *are being* sanctified (14). How do you tie together the time-frame here?
2. In what ways did Jesus do the will of God? And who are the 'enemies' (13) who are not yet submitted to him?
3. Why is it 'impossible for the blood of bulls and goats to take away sins' (4)? What is it about bulls and goats that makes this impossible? And what is it about the sacrifice of Jesus' body (10) that works?

10:15–31

On the doorstep of heaven

The final, unrepeatable sacrifice of Jesus is our hope and joy, as we rejoice in the witness of the Spirit in our hearts and stand together on the very threshold of the Most Holy Place.

There are three little sections in this passage, as the author draws threads together and looks back to the starting-point of his main argument in chapter 4.
The three sections are held together by the thought of the *unrepeatability* of the sacrifice of Jesus ('there is no longer any offering', 'no sacrifice for sins is left', 26).

First, *he encourages us with the witness of the Holy Spirit* (15–18). The Jeremiah passage quoted in Hebrews 8 has never been far from his thoughts, and here he returns to it explicitly. But what exactly is the witness of the Holy Spirit? Is it just these words, written by Jeremiah under the inspiration of the Spirit?

We have to read very carefully here. The quotation is introduced with 'First he says', leading us, of course, to expect something like 'Then he adds …'. But in the Greek this never comes, apparently. The NIV has inserted it in verse 17, just to make sense of the passage. But this is not necessary. We should translate it like this: 'For after saying, "This is the covenant I will make with them after those days", the Lord then says, "I will put my laws in their hearts, and write them on their minds, and I will remember their sins and transgressions no more." '

There is a 'the Lord says' *within the quotation*, which the author cleverly exploits. This means that the witness of the Spirit is not the words uttered by Jeremiah, but the experience prophesied by Jeremiah, the inner experience of renewal and forgiveness. Unlike the worshippers of old, who never lost their inner 'conscience' of sin, however often the Day of Atonement took place (10:1–2), we do experience a deep inner sense of forgiveness and a knowledge that the Lord has renewed us within by his Spirit. There's a love for him and a desire to obey him – to do his will, in fact, like Jesus (10:7). We know that the sacrifice of Christ has worked. So we can agree that it does not need to be repeated (18).

Secondly, *he urges us to take worship seriously* (19–25). This is a most marvellous passage, often used in worship – quite rightly. Since he has written so much about Old Testament worship, we'd expect the author to have something to say about worship under the new covenant. And he does. But there are hidden depths here. He continues to use the symbolism of the Day of Atonement, and imagines us following Jesus, our 'great priest' (21), into the Most Holy Place, through the veil that separates this world from 'the heavens' (see 4:14). This looks back to 6:19, where he called Jesus our forerunner, thus introducing the very surprising idea that this high priest does not enter alone into the Holy of Holies. The veil, says our author appropriately, is not the physical one in the temple, but the flesh of Jesus, his broken body. This becomes the 'crossover point', the intersection, the border zone between this world and 'the heavens', where God dwells.

We can 'draw near', like the high priest approaching the veil on the Day. In verse 22 the author uses ordination language, drawn from Exodus 29:4 and Leviticus 16:4; it's as though we too have been ordained to priesthood, like Aaron and his sons, and now we draw near to the Holy of Holies, ready to enter, like them. Clearly, the reference to water suggests baptism, but the author of Hebrews gives us a new perspective on baptism here: think of it as ordination. To worship on the threshold of heaven, we need to be cleansed in conscience (22), confident in faith (23), active in love (24), and committed to fellowship (25) – because 'the Day' truly is drawing near.

Thirdly, *he warns us not to fall away* (26–31). These verses look back to the warning passages in 6:4–6 and 2:1–4. This is what the author fears for his readers. If they slip back into being 'just Jews', then they will have decided that Jesus is not essential to salvation. And even if they don't express contempt for Jesus as in verse 29, they will nevertheless be throwing their lot in with others who do, and committing themselves to belong to a group that regards Jesus' blood, not as the inauguration of a new covenant, but as 'common', that is, just like any other sample of human blood. Even though his blood once 'sanctified' them (29), they've rejected it. What's more, they will be insulting the Spirit of grace (29), the Holy Spirit who has given special charismatic gifts to them, on which they now turn their backs and say, 'No, thanks.'

This is the other side of the point about the unrepeatability of Jesus' sacrifice. There's nowhere else to go. Verse 26 alludes to the story of the sons of Eli, who stood just where we are – on the doorstep of the sanctuary – and sinned 'high-handedly' against the Lord, exploiting the worshippers and having sex with the serving girls. Though warned, they persisted, and so the word came through Samuel: 'The guilt of Eli's house will never be atoned for by sacrifice or offering' (1 Samuel 3:14). Jesus sets us free 'to serve the living God' (9:14), but it's also 'a dreadful thing to fall into the hands of the living God' (10:31), and if we've finally rejected

Jesus, then what way back is there? We shall end up at odds with God himself.

Questions

1. Is it ever right to conclude that any particular person is in the state described in verses 29–31?
2. Do we really 'enter the Most Holy Place' (19) in worship – that is, go right into the presence of God himself? Or is this reserved for 'the Day' (25), either of our death, or of the second coming?
3. What would you say to someone who felt that they'd lost the witness of the Spirit – someone who has no conviction of inner renewal and is still very conscious of their sins, feeling lots of guilt?

10:32–39

Hang on in there!

A final exhortation rounds off the central section of the letter. Life is tough for the followers of Jesus. We need each other, and we need him.

The author is desperate to encourage his Hebrews. He wants to raise their spirits and their zeal – to 'strengthen their feeble arms and weak knees', as he puts it later (12:12). He could jump straight into the honours gallery in chapter 11, but just hearing about other people's courage and faith can actually be discouraging: we think, 'I can't be like that!' Far more encouraging, in fact, is to be reminded that we've managed it ourselves already. We did it before; maybe we can do it again!

That's what the author does in these verses. He reminds the readers of their early Christian experience, when they faced a great deal of hardship and persecution. His implication is that it may be necessary to do it again – but isn't it worth it? Let's look as some of the details.

Verse 32: 'you stood your ground in a great contest in the face of suffering'. He uses 'athletics' language here, as Paul does too, about his sufferings (1 Corinthians 9:25–27), and as the author will again, very dramatically, in 12:1–4.

Verses 33–34: 'you were publicly exposed to insult and persecution … you stood side by side with those who were so treated … you sympathised with those in prison'. This is all about *shame*. Ancient Greek and Roman culture – the dominant culture within which the readers lived – was based on 'honour' and 'shame' values. Social life was all about how to achieve honour in the sight of your fellow human beings, and the worst thing that could happen to you was to be shamed in some way. Here the expression 'publicly exposed' is the giveaway. It became a matter of public shame to be identified as a Christian. But they bore it – and not only so, but voluntarily incurred more shame by deliberately associating with their fellow Christians who were likewise shamed or even imprisoned for their faith.

This reference to association with prisoners is very telling. To be imprisoned was in itself to incur shame, whatever the cause. How could it bring you honour, under any circumstances? And to associate with prisoners (to visit them and bring them food – there was no prison food in those days) meant becoming infected with their shame. This is why some Christians in Rome did not want to associate with Paul the prisoner; see Philippians 1:15–18.

The most dreadful shame of all, of course – bringing shame upon you, everything you stood for, your whole life, your family, friends and all associated with you – was to be crucified.

Verse 34: 'you … joyfully accepted the confiscation of your property, because you knew that you yourselves had better and lasting possessions'. A court or local official might have imposed hefty fines on them, or there could have been mob justice, looting their homes and property. Either way, it must have been a terrible thing to bear – but they did. And it was their *theology* that sustained them at that time. They knew that to possess Jesus and to treasure in him was worth far more than all earthly treasure.

So they've managed it before. This brings the author to his final exhortation, backed up with a scriptural quotation, in verses 35–39. Don't throw away your 'confidence', or, boldness, he says (35). This word 'confidence' last appeared in 10:19, where they were told that they could have 'confidence to enter the Most Holy Place' because of Jesus. Actually, they go together: confidence to trust in Jesus means confidence to follow him through suffering, if he calls us. The author also used this word twice on the other side of the central section of his letter, in a way that balances its two appearances here – see 3:6 and 4:16. I think this is probably deliberate. The end of verse 35 suggests that they have already earned a rich reward for their earlier confidence – don't lose it by failing to keep going now! They have before them the example of Jesus, who has brought about such a wonderful result by doing the will of God (10:7, 10); now it's their turn, if necessary, to do God's will by suffering like Jesus, so that through their perseverance they too may 'receive what he [God] has promised', like Abraham (36; compare 6:15).

Then comes the final quotation, from Habakkuk 2:3–4, which tells them that they may not have to wait very long. This is a good example of a quotation that the author takes from the Greek Bible, the Septuagint, and which differs quite a bit from the Hebrew at this point. And, in fact, the author has swapped it around a little, too. He was probably quoting it from memory. He makes it an exhortation not to shrink back from the challenge, or compromise their commitment, but to have faith, the faith by which the righteous live, according to Habakkuk – because the coming one is on his way, and will soon be here. The Day is dawning. There's not long to wait.

These final themes – faith, endurance, perseverance, looking ahead for the coming one – lead into the tour through the honours gallery that is our next treat.

Questions

1. How do you keep going when everything seems to be going wrong and the whole world is against you?
2. How can we better support Christians in countries where persecution happens all the time? In what practical ways can we encourage them?
3. How much 'confidence' do you think you have as a Christian – thinking of all four verses where this word comes in Hebrews (3:6; 4:16; 10:19; 10:35)? What could others do, to help you grow in confidence?
4. Looking back over the whole central part of the letter, 4:14 – 10:39, what do you think God has taught you above all? Is there one particular thing, or many? What are they?

Digging deeper: The atonement in Hebrews

It's worth pausing to reflect a little about the atonement, because it is such an important topic. We can draw together the threads of our study of Hebrews as we do so. Basically, there are seven points to make about 'the atonement in Hebrews', two negative and five positive.

First, it is remarkable that Hebrews does not present the atonement in terms of justice and punishment. This is how it is often presented today, but it is not what we find in Hebrews. We touched on this when we were looking at 10:7–10, in connection with the unity between the Father and the Son in the atonement (see above, page 125). There is no division between them, with the Father making demands (for necessary justice and punishment) and the

Son fulfilling those demands. The broader point to make, alongside this point about unity, is that the language of 'justice' and 'punishment' simply fails to appear in Hebrews. However our author thinks of atonement, it is not that God required the death of Jesus as the just punishment for our sins. He never says this. Interesting!

Secondly, Hebrews does not present God as subject to some kind of 'law' outside himself, which determines how atonement must be made. This is an important point, because it is often maintained in connection with 9:22 that here we have the basic principle that determines how atonement must be achieved and why death is necessary – 'without the shedding of blood there is no forgiveness'. Here's a kind of rule, we are told, which requires the shedding of Jesus' blood on the cross – a rule like the 'magic from beyond the dawn of time' in C. S. Lewis's *The Lion, the Witch and the Wardrobe*. But the author of Hebrews is too great a theologian to be satisfied with simply accepting a bald 'principle' like that. He would ask, as we do, *Why*? In the Old Testament, as we have seen, there are numerous examples of God forgiving people without the shedding of blood, so why does the author of Hebrews come up with this statement? It can't be that there is some binding 'law' of atonement to which God is subject. Of course God decides how he will make atonement for our sins, and it involved the shedding of Jesus' blood for us – but why? Why could he not just forgive us?

This brings us to our four positive points. Thirdly, at the heart of the atonement lies Jesus' sharing in our humanity, our 'flesh and blood'. This is where Hebrews starts, in chapter 2, as we saw. That chapter is wonderfully moving in its picture of the incarnation of the Son of God. In Hebrews, the incarnation is not just the essential preliminary to the 'real' work of atonement, which is Jesus' death on the cross. The incarnation is the primary act in atonement. Atonement is 'at-one-ment' – it's all about how we become 'at one' again with God. And we saw in chapter 2 how the whole thing starts from that remarkable statement in 2:11, that 'the one who sanctifies and those who are sanctified are "of one"' (my translation). Atonement starts with the recognition that there already is an 'at-one-ness' between us and the heavenly Son of God, because we all share the 'image' of God. That sharing is then made concrete as he assumes 'flesh and blood' and becomes exactly like us (yes, that's what Hebrews says) – apart from sinning, of course.

Fourthly, this is why Jesus' death is at the heart of the atonement in Hebrews: because, sharing our flesh and blood, he must die. His flesh was mortal flesh. Hebrews is clear that he was tried exactly as we are, in every way (4:15) – and then gives, as the supreme example of this, his trial before his death (5:7–8). United with us in flesh and blood, he went through everything that we have to face. This is why his death was an offering of himself – his whole incarnation was. And that's why the author sets the emphasis where he does in chapter 10 – 'a body you pre-pared for me … I have come to do your will, O God' (10:5–7). He does not come like the old, mechanical sacri-fices, performed meticulously by rote year after year, but on an entirely new basis, through a new doing of God's will, by sharing our full humanity and therefore dying with us. But how does this achieve atonement?

Fifthly, atonement works in Hebrews because the fel-lowship both between the Father and the Son, and between the Son and humankind, remains unbroken. Although he was the Son of God, he 'learned obedience from what he suffered' (5:8), thus deepening his union with his Father – if this were possible. And through the very same act he became eligible to be 'designated … high priest' (5:10), an office for which he has to be human – high priests are selected from among humans (5:1). So his death deepens and enlarges his union both with us, and with his Father – and means that, when he returns to the 'Most Holy Place', heaven, he does so *as high priest*, repre-senting us, still united with us, and symbolizing his union with us by bringing his blood with him. This is powerful stuff indeed!

Sixthly, the essence of atonement is thus the experience

of unity with God in Christ. Here Hebrews makes powerful use of the notion of 'cleansing the sanctuary'. As we saw, this strange idea arises from the closeness of God to his people. When they sin, he is affected, because he is alongside them. So, symbolically, the sanctuary must be 'cleansed'. The author of Hebrews doesn't abandon this idea, but applies it to the heavenly sanctuary, because he believes that it is not far away. There is no 'great gulf fixed' between heaven and earth. We saw this again in 10:19–25, where the author encourages us to think of ourselves as on the very doorstep of heaven when we worship. We stand on holy ground, because Jesus gives us access to the sanctuary, and we have 'confidence to enter'. The church tastes the gifts of heaven and the powers of the coming age (6:4–5). They are very close!

Already, therefore, because of Jesus, we enter into atonement, the experience of union with God, especially in our worship. (But in Hebrews 'worship' is not just what we do when we meet to pray – see 13:15–16.) Jesus makes it truly possible for us to enjoy the presence of God – both now and hereafter.

Finally (point no. 7), we can see what Hebrews means by making purification for sins in 1:3. The NIV is misleading, I think, when it uses the word 'providing' instead of 'making'. 'Providing' suggests that Jesus has made it available – it's there on the stall in the market, and we can go and get it if we'd like some. But, as we saw, 'make' means much more than 'make available'. It's a creation word, parallel to making the universe in 1:2. Sin is that which wrecks the relationship between God and the world he made. But that relationship has been restored by his Son, who became incarnate within his world and, as one of us, has returned to his Father's right hand. Heaven and earth have been reunited (at-oned). So if we have Jesus as our champion, our high priest, then he will be the 'source of eternal salvation' (5:9) for us too.

EYES ON THE PRIZE

Hebrews 11:1 – 12:29

Stop and look: The story of faith

The author has said it all, actually, at this point. But it's a measure of his love for his readers that he doesn't cut and run, sign off and go out for a pizza. He gives them – and us – one of the most moving and powerful conclusions to a letter ever written – three more chapters of it.

In theory, yes, the argument is complete at this point. But the whole story has not been told. He's given them the theology that should persuade them that Jesus is the essential fulfilment of the Old Testament covenant and hope, which are incomplete without him. But he hasn't been completely fair to the Old Testament in the process. He's treated it as a theological source – revelation from God, to be reassessed in the light of the 'new word' spoken through the Son (2:3–4). But he hasn't treated it as a human drama, which is what it also is. The Old Testament is also the story of the people who heard God, trusted him, loved, messed up, won through, and bore testimony to his power and grace. And of course that is where the readers identify themselves – they are the people of the covenant, one with the 'fathers' and 'elders' who have gone before. For them, there's a great demand of loyalty exerted by their connection with this ancestry. They can't just throw all that away – and, in fact, that's probably what generates the most powerful argument, keeping them where they are, in the synagogue and the theology it represents. It's always the personal, 'people' factors that weigh most highly. We can talk theology until we're blue in the face, but we'll go wherever the heart pulls us.

So it's vital for the readers to feel that their community with their ancestors is not broken if they decide to go with the author and his theology. If it feels like disloyalty they won't buy into it. That's the purpose of the next two chapters – not just chapter 11, but chapter 12 as well. The author wants to show that their forefathers and 'ancients' are like a great crowd of spectators, cheering them on and waving enthusiastically, as they hold on to Jesus – not tut-tutting and shaking their heads in sorrow. And he wants to show that it's all one story – the story of the forefathers, continued into the story of Jesus, and then further into their story, the followers of Jesus – it's all one seamless narrative, heading towards one glorious conclusion. How could they bear not to be part of it?

I've talked here about 'forefathers' and 'ancients' because that is how the readers would refer to them. But here's another interesting observation; the author of Hebrews avoids these descriptions of the characters in the honours gallery. He refers just once to 'our forefathers', in 1:1, and never again; and just once to 'the ancients' in 11:2. Apart from that, he simply refers to these characters by name – no honorific titles. The implication? We are to think of them just as people – people like us, with ordinary human names, facing real, human situations.

We are going to read chapter 11 in two long chunks, because it's meant to make a broad impression rather than be studied in minute detail. (We have to remember that the New Testament letters were written to be read out to the assembled church rather than duplicated and distributed to each church member.) The author concentrates on the early period, the period before the law was given, and he separates it into two instalments, with a commentary in between:

11:1–3	Introduction
11:4–12	Abel to Abraham: how to die in faith
11:13–16	Commentary: not receiving the promises, aliens and strangers on earth
11:17–38	Abraham to Eliazar: how to live by faith
11:39–40	Commentary: not receiving the promises, waiting for us

Then chapter 12 takes the story on to Jesus, and the readers, as we shall see, and looks ahead to the end of the story in the fulfilment of the longing for home that gripped the earliest fathers. The author refers back to Abel again, in

12:24, rounding the whole story off, and concludes with the final exhortation that burns in his heart.

11:1–16

How to die in faith

Faith is real, practical, and everyday. It's not an intellectual, mind-focused thing, or a set of truths to believe. It's tough, it's sensitive, it's realistic, and it's otherworldly. In fact –

Faith is that inner grasp on the things you hope for, all the proof you need of things you can't see (1, my translation). This verse, introducing the whole chapter, is a practical definition of faith – more a definition of believing than of 'faith' in the abstract. This is what faith meant to the characters who now parade in front of us, and it's what faith will mean for us, too. It's vital for the author to show his readers that he's asking them to believe in just the same way as the great 'ancients' (2) of Israel. In fact, he shows the ancients believing in a way that matches the theology of Hebrews 1–10 – looking forward to the 'real thing' yet to be, not rejoicing that they had everything already in the old covenant, law and cult.

'Promise' – that's the vital word, as we'll see. The people of God live by the word of God, responding to it in whatever way is appropriate. That's true for new-covenant people as much as for old-covenant people.

Verse 3 also prepares the way for the whole chapter, because it expresses the presupposition with which we read these old stories. We presuppose a world in which 'the word of God' is the decisive creative factor, and in which reality does not always appear: things are some-

times very different from the way they look. The NRSV
translation is better here – 'what is seen was made from
things that are not visible'. There's a whole 'not visible'
reality, lurking under the surface, but summoning us and
visible to faith (see verse 1); and on the basis of this 'not
visible reality' we live our lives and interpret the lives of
others. We believe that Jesus the Son of God sustains all
things by his powerful word (1:3).

So the author launches into his roll of merit in the
gallery of faith. First we have *Abel* (4), who anticipated the
sacrificial system in worship but reveals through the terrible conflict with his brother that it's the heart that makes
the difference in offering sacrifices. Without faith, that real
'seeing' of the unseen God, all worship is vain.

Then we have *Enoch* (5–6), who also reveals how vital
faith is to worship. His faith in the unseen God was so
strong that he simply bypassed death. He had learned
how to please God, and faith was vital to that. No true
worship (coming or drawing near to God, 6) is possible
without true faith.

And then *Noah* (7): he too responded to the word of God
about unseen realities, and launched out in faith – literally! But his faith-launch anticipated the arrival of the water
by many years.

Then comes *Abraham* (8–12), a great favourite of our
author. He has already referred to him in chapters 6 and 7;
he's at the heart of the Melchizedek episode. Here the
author picks up the nomadic quality of Abraham's life.
He'd received huge promises of greatness (Genesis 12:1–3;
15:1–6, etc.), which we heard about in 6:14, but he never
lived to see them fulfilled. What kept him going? The
author concludes: it must have been the vision of the wonderful thing that God would do to fulfil his promise: 'he
was looking forward to the city with foundations, whose
architect and builder is God' (10) – a real, solid city, with
real foundations, unlike this flimsy tent. But the city was
visible only with the eyes of faith.

Verse 11, I think, should have Sarah as its subject. (The
translation is a bit difficult.) Abraham's wife is not to be

left out. 'By faith Sarah, even though she was barren, received the power to conceive well past the normal time, because she considered him faithful who had promised' (my translation). *We* know how it all turned out – verse 12! – but Abraham and Sarah never saw it. For them, it was just promise. But look back to 10:23: our faith has the same shape to it, resting on God's promise and his 'faithfulness' to it.

This leads into the first 'commentary' in verses 13–16. These patriarchs all knew that something wonderful was coming. Their faith convinced them of it – that faith which is 'that inner grasp on the things you hope for, all the proof you need of things you can't see' (1, my translation). They were 'longing for a better country – a heavenly one' (16). Why 'heavenly'? Here we run into the author's conception of 'heaven'. Remember that, for him, it is not far away. Heaven interpenetrates this world. It's the unseen reality lying just behind the appearance of things. So, even if these patriarchs had expected a solid, earthly city – one with real foundations – it would also be 'heavenly' because God would be involved in it, its 'architect and builder' (10). The result is that during their lives they were 'aliens and strangers on earth' (13), not fitting in, because they saw things differently and lived by a different vision. It was their relationship with God, solidified by their faith, that made them so different from the world around. And they hung on to their faith right through death – never receiving the promises, but believing in them right to the moment of their passing.

Questions

1. List for yourself the difficulties and challenges that make believing hard for you in your circumstances. Imagine yourself in conversation with Abraham about them. What do you say to each other? (NB: be real.)
2. Is it right for believers to feel like 'aliens and strangers' on the earth (13)? Shouldn't we feel at home here, since

we know who made it and believe that he's put us here for a purpose? Do you feel like an alien and stranger?

3. Do you think that we have now entered into the fulfilment of the promises that Abraham was looking forward to? Have we 'received' them? (Remember your thoughts about this question – it's vital for later in Hebrews.)

4. What are the promises of God that mean a lot to you? Which do you specially hold on to?

11:17–40

How to live by faith

The honours list continues with a roll-call of the great adventurers of faith. This is how to be a superb human being, someone too good for this earth, of whom 'the world was not worthy'.

The first part of the list featured four 'specials' from Genesis – Abel, Enoch, Noah and Abraham. The second part now features fourteen, from the rest of the Old Testament and beyond, in two groups of seven: seven named and described (17–31), and then seven named as typical of many more (32–38). The focus on 'seven' is probably deliberate, precisely because it underlines their perfection (see the last word of the chapter, 11:40) while at the same time opening them up for us to copy. They're not a closed club. The list is open-ended, as the second 'seven' make very clear.

We start with Abraham again (17–19), this time in his sacrifice of Isaac. The author has already alluded to this story in 6:14, as we saw. Abraham goes with Isaac (20),

Jacob (21), and Joseph (22), forming a group who together show how faith is focused on God's future. All of them are concerned with death, and with seeing God's future beyond the grave. Abraham was willing to sacrifice Isaac – and because he knew that Isaac was the son of promise, he knew also that somehow Isaac would be preserved, by resurrection if necessary. Isaac blessed his sons Jacob and Esau in a way that deliberately shaped the future for both of them (Genesis 27). On his deathbed Jacob did the same thing for Ephraim and Manasseh, the sons of Joseph, turning them into full tribes of Israel (Genesis 48:8–20). And then Joseph, dying in Egypt, explicitly looked forward to the exodus and the return to the promised land (Genesis 50:24–26).

And then Moses (23–29). He gets four 'by faiths' as the author summarizes his amazing life – the same number as Abraham (more than Abraham, if verse 11 goes to Sarah). The author knows that he will be accused by his Jewish critics – maybe even by the readers – of downplaying Moses and undermining his significance in God's plan. He wants to make it clear that he does no such thing. But, interestingly, he passes through Moses' career without mentioning his role as receiver of the law for Israel. This happens between verses 29 and 30. He mentioned it twice during his main argument (7:14 and 9:19), but on both occasions it was to mark Moses as mediator of the old covenant, now renewed in Christ. Here, however, he wants to make him an example of new-covenant faith, the kind of faith he wants his readers to have – not faith in the law, but faith in the Christ.

Rather than just faith in the future, Moses' faith ventures are all concerned with faith in action against danger and the threats of enemies – this is real hero-book stuff! The author even mentions 'Christ' in verse 26, in a most interesting way. Probably he doesn't mean that Moses was aware that he was suffering for Jesus when he decided to give up being an Egyptian prince and throw in his lot with his own people (Exodus 2:11–15). Literally, 'he considered the reproach of the Christ greater riches than all the treasures of Egypt' – in other words, he was willing to accept the shame of giving up his position as prince of Egypt and taking on the role of 'the Christ' for his people. He became their anointed deliverer, and from then on his life was nothing but trouble. In delivering Israel from Egypt he foreshadowed the one who will deliver Israel again – from death (2:14–18).

The three 'by faiths' in verses 29–31 are also all risks taken against danger and death. Rahab is boldly called 'the prostitute' because she illustrates how it's not obedience to the law that brings us into relationship with God, but faith – venturesome, extravagant, foolish, obedient faith. In fact, all these seven named 'by faiths' are concerned with facing and overcoming death. That's the hallmark of faith in 'the living God' (9:14) – it's life-giving. Even in old-covenant times, the new-covenant gift of victory over death (2:14–18) was being experienced and expressed.

And that's the note that carries on ringing in the second seven, the open set that moves right up to the present (32–38). It's a stirring description of faith heroics and devotion – interestingly drawing quite a lot on the experiences of the Maccabees, the Jewish freedom-fighters who opposed the tyranny of the Syrian empire over Israel in the second century BC. The seven sons of Eleazar were famous for submitting to martyrdom, alongside their father, rather than bowing to the emperor's demands. The first readers will have noticed how some of the descriptions here refer to the exploits and sufferings of the Maccabees for their faith. This is important – it brings it up to date. These are not just Old Testament figures, set in stained glass, divorced from present life and somehow capable of far more than us. The Maccabees were recent history. And we could add to this list from modern Christian biography as well. Faith does move mountains, even if the world doesn't recognize it. The author's careful writing is evident in verses 33–34, where he lists nine great mountains moved by faith, in three groups of three – three great achievements, three marvellous deliverances, and three feats of strength. Once again, the facing and overcoming of death is the keynote of this faith – and, along with death, the willing embracing of shame in the eyes of society.

The concluding commentary in verses 39–40 is so evocative. All these ventures of faith were done on the basis of a vision – a vision of what will yet be, in the plan of God, a promise yet to be fulfilled. None of the people mentioned saw the full vision (just parts of it – verses 33–34). The whole point was that they should reach that 'perfection' with us, says the author. Precisely because we and they belong together, we shall all reach the city together. This is just what his readers need to know – that they will deepen their fellowship with their forefathers through following Jesus.

Questions

1. Can you add any stories of modern faith to the honours roll-call? What stories would you particularly tell? Who are your heroes of faith?
2. What kind of fellowship do we enjoy now with the great believers of the past? Do we just remember them, or are we still in communion with them in some way? (There's a 'Digging deeper' box on this following – but what do you think?)
3. Write your own obituary! This rather sober-sounding suggestion can be a very good exercise for thinking through exactly what you want your priorities to be and how you want to be remembered. How big a role will 'by faith' play in your obituary?

Digging deeper: Family across eternity

The last verse of chapter 11 is very suggestive: 'God had planned something better for us so that only together with us would they be made perfect.' 'Not apart from us' (literally) – what does this mean?

The author develops this thought through the picture in 12:1–2 of the 'great cloud of witnesses' surrounding us and cheering us on as we run the race. I am writing this just before the 2004 Olympic Games are due to begin in Athens, Greece. The image the author uses here is drawn from the original Olympics. The running track was not oval, as now, but long and narrow. Competitors would run down one side, wheel around a post at the far end, and then hurtle back again. The result of this was that the spectators were much closer – the runners would go right past twice on every 'lap'. Incidentally, they ran naked, which the author picks up here in his reference to 'throwing off everything that hinders'.

Who are the spectators? They are, of course, all the 'heroes' of chapter 11. They are witnesses, not just in that they testify to the power of faith through the stories of their lives – their exploits of faith – but also in that they are in the stands, witnessing our efforts to do the same. They reappear in 12:23, the marvellous concluding passage where the author lists all the things to which we have 'drawn near' through faith in Jesus. We've drawn near not just to him (he's items 7 and 8 in the list), but also to the assembly of the firstborn who are enrolled in heaven, and to the spirits of the righteous made perfect. Within the sweep of the letter, we know who these are – we needn't cast around for further definitions. 'The firstborn' might be particularly the earliest patriarchs, the ones on whom chapter 11 concentrates. But, together, these two phrases clearly cover the whole company of the 'dead in Christ', of both old and new covenants, those who have 'gone before' in their life of faith and in their death without receiving the promise.

We have 'drawn near' to them; they are 'witnesses' surrounding us; we are to 'be made perfect' together – it sounds as though the author has a healthy sense of the unity of the one church of Jesus Christ, which consists both of the church on earth and of the church already in heaven. This is a strong theme in Orthodox theology, which emphasizes this one fellowship of the redeemed, united in worship – and this then influences the Orthodox theology of worship quite profoundly. When we worship here on earth, we are joining the worship of heaven, and our expression is united with the expression of praise uttered by those who have gone before us into the blessed place.

Is this true? Is this how Hebrews would encourage us to think?

To some extent this depends on the answer to one of the questions asked above, after the study on 10:19–25: the question was, 'Do we really "enter the Most Holy Place" in worship … Or is this reserved for "the Day" (25), either of our death, or of the second coming?' Asking this question of successive generations of students at London School of Theology, I get mixed responses. Some, influenced by the use of worship songs drawn from the book of Revelation, say, 'Yes, of course we enter the Most Holy Place when we worship – we go right into the presence of God.' It certainly seems to be true of Revelation: if we sing the songs recorded in Revelation 4 – 5, then we are joining the worship of heaven itself.

But others reply, 'Ah! Singing the songs doesn't necessarily mean entering the place! Here in Hebrews we're standing on the threshold to worship, not yet entering the Holy of Holies.' To which the first group respond, 'But in Hebrews 12 we've drawn so near that the author can say that "you have come" to Mount Zion, and he can describe in detail the people we've joined there.'

Probably both groups have truth on their side. The author certainly wants us to feel one with 'the saints in glory', but obviously we can't be one with them now in the same way as we shall be one with them after death, or when the 'enduring city' arrives (13:14). Then, there will be an intimacy of union that won't be broken by the river of death flowing in between. But, having said that, we are certainly one with them in Christ; and we are all, they and we together, looking forward to the final consummation, the city that is to come, when together we will be perfected in Christ.

For we are in just the same situation as the saints of the old covenant; it's not that we've entered the fulfilment of the promises they were looking forward to. 'We see Jesus' (1:9), but we're still looking forward, like them, to the unshakable kingdom yet to be (12:28).

How is our fellowship with them made concrete? In Roman Catholic tradition we are encouraged to pray to them and to believe that they pray for us – but it has to be said that this goes beyond biblical evidence. However, we can certainly celebrate their memory, rejoice in our continued union with them in Christ, believe that in worship we are especially close to them, and look forward to being (re)united with them one day in glory. And, on top of that, maybe we can imagine them, as Hebrews does, looking on and cheering as we try to live faithfully in our day, as they did in theirs.

12:1–17

Heaven's children

Jesus' life of faith completes the honours catalogue, but also 'perfects' it because he is so great. He becomes our great champion, encouraging us to keep going in the race, however tough it is.

The honours list in chapter 11 is bracketed by the idea of 'endurance'. It comes in 10:32, 36 (NIV, 'stood your ground', 'persevere'), summarizing what the 'Hebrews' need in the face of all the challenges ahead. Now it appears again in 12:1–3, 7 ('perseverance', 'endure[d]'), describing again what the Hebrews need (1, 7), and also what Jesus himself displayed when he faced the cross (2, 3). These are the only places where this word is used in Hebrews, so the author chooses it deliberately as a way of summarizing what the list is all about, and how we should respond to it. Endurance is that quality of faith which manifests itself in patience and joy under suffering. The heroes had it, we need it, and Jesus above all displayed it.

In a sense Jesus therefore brings the honours list to a conclusion – but not really. 'Climax' would be a better word than 'conclusion', for the list is open-ended, and the author wants his readers' names on there as well. So they too must 'endure' (12:7), and he will tell them how. Jesus is 'the champion and perfecter of our faith' (2, my translation), its ultimate exponent. And it is on the cross that we see faith supremely displayed: 'who for the joy set before him endured the cross, scorning its shame, and sat down at the right hand of the throne of God'. Here we have Psalm 110 again, deliberately now contrasting the destination of the journey with the route. In order to arrive at God's right hand, Jesus went through crucifixion. In a little 'Digging deeper' section below, I've given a quotation from Professor Martin Hengel, of Tübingen University, illustrating what crucifixion meant in the ancient world. It was the ultimate degradation. To go from that to the ultimate glorification, intimately linking the two, so that Jesus comes to the glory because he went through the shame – that's the 'faith' of our Lord Jesus Christ.

Keep going in the footsteps of Jesus, looking to him (2), says the author. A very similar phrase, 'looking to God', is given as the tombstone inscription for the seven sons of Eleazar in the fourth book of Maccabees. Jewish readers might notice the change here: for us, *Jesus* is now the focus of our devotion and dedication. He's our inspiration as we face all the challenges and trials of our lives.

That's the author's focus now. In the rest of this passage, he encourages us to join the honours list by learning the secret of 'faith' for ourselves. What's the secret? It has three parts to it, all very simple.

First, *keep your eyes on Jesus* (3–4). Simply considering how Jesus endured such 'opposition' (or 'hostility', NRSV) can have a wonderfully encouraging effect – 'so that you will not grow weary and lose heart'. The author's words are so simple, but so profound. We need to be able to face the worst that life can bring, without losing heart. And we probably won't have to go as far as Jesus did: 'In your struggle against sin, you have not yet resisted to the point of shedding your blood' (4). This is not a threat but an encouragement: if Jesus could endure all that, then you can put up with less, surely!

Secondly, *learn to belong to Father* (5–11). This follows on. Where did Jesus gain the strength? From his relationship with his Father. And you're in exactly the same relationship, says our author. Taking a quotation from Proverbs 3:11–12, he develops the theme of 'discipline' or (a better translation) 'education'. Every father wants to bring up his children, to educate them into mature adulthood. Such education can be really painful, but it's a completely necessary process if childhood is to be left behind. Remember: the author told us that Jesus himself, the Son of God, went through just such a process of education, 'learning obedience' from suffering (5:7–8). How can we avoid it ourselves? Every painful experience we face can be seen as part of the process, part of our Father's 'education' of us as his children – and proof that he cares for us.

Thirdly, *look after each other* (12–17). It's important to realize that these verses are a community exhortation. It's not 'strengthen your [own, individual] feeble arms and weak knees' (12), but 'strengthen each other's feeble arms and weak knees'. We all need to strengthen each other for the race that lies ahead (the 'athletics' metaphor continues from verses 1–2). None of us has enough strength, on our own. The opening encouragement in verse 15, 'See to it that …', would better be translated, 'Watch over each other lest …' The Greek for 'watch over' is the word from which we get 'overseer' or 'bishop'. We need to exercise episcopal care of each other, because we can't get there alone. On our own, injuries become disabilities (13). But with others caring for us, they get healed.

There's a lot at stake. Without this sort of care, we might 'miss the grace of God' (15). This word 'miss' was used in 4:1 about missing God's rest (the NIV translates it 'fallen short' there). In both cases it's a serious warning. God's grace isn't a guarantee, in Hebrews. It's available at 'the throne of grace' (4:16) – but if we decide we don't need the high priest, we won't get to the throne, and so we could miss the grace. Verse 15 includes sobering language, drawn from Deuteronomy 29:18, about the way the Israelites were meant to take care of each other, lest someone in their midst should start going astray after other gods.

This really is tough – and ironic. The readers are tempted to think that, by stepping back from Jesus and being 'just Jews', they would be proving their faithfulness to Jacob and the covenant that God made with him. But no; they'd actually be like Esau, Jacob's renegade brother, who denied the covenant for a single quick meal. And, the author tells them, watch out (for each other); he wasn't allowed back once he'd taken that irrevocable step (16–17).

There's a 'Digging deeper' section on Esau below (pages 154–157). Why could he 'find no chance to repent' (NRSV)?

Questions

1. Can you see how God has 'educated' you, as his child, through the painful experiences you've had to bear? What did you learn? Share some testimonies with others.
2. 'On our own, injuries become disabilities (13). But with others caring for us, they get healed.' Can you think of ways in which this works out in practice? How could fellowship become more real and effective in this kind of 'mutual oversight'?
3. (This needs a group.) Why not turn verses 1–2 into a

dramatic presentation, using whatever gifts are available in your group? Acting, painting, music, poetry, storytelling – why not do it all through the eyes of one of the 'witnesses' in the cheering crowd?

Digging deeper: Crucifixion

This quotation from Martin Hengel's book *Crucifixion* (SCM, 1977, pages 86–88) illustrates especially its shame, the emphasis also placed on it by Hebrews:

Crucifixion was and remained a political and military punishment. While among the Persians and the Carthaginians it was imposed primarily on high officials and commanders, as on rebels, among the Romans it was inflicted above all on the lower classes, i.e. slaves, violent criminals, and the unruly elements in rebellious provinces, not least in Judaea ... As a rule the crucified man was regarded as a criminal who was receiving just and necessary punishment ... It was usually associated with other forms of torture, including at least flogging. At relatively small expense and to great public effect the criminal could be tortured to death for days in an unspeakable way ... By the public display of a naked victim at a prominent place – at a crossroads, in the theatre, on high ground, at the place of his crime – crucifixion represented his uttermost humiliation ... Crucifixion was aggravated further by the fact that quite often its victims were never buried. It was a stereotyped picture that the crucified victim served as food for wild beasts and birds of prey. In this way his humiliation was made complete. What it meant for a man in antiquity to be refused burial, and the dishonour which went with it, can hardly be appreciated by modern man.

This is the death that Jesus, the Son of God, chose to die for us, so that no-one could claim to have sunk lower than he, and therefore to escape the reach of his association with our 'flesh and blood'. And through this, to the right hand of God! This is the kind of love that God honours.

Digging deeper: Esau and his tears: why no second chance?

At first sight it seems so unfair and unmerciful. Is this really the God we know in Jesus? Apparently Esau wanted to repent, but 'found no place' (literally) for it. It seems as though his repentance wasn't allowed space before God, wasn't valid, evoked no forgiveness of his sin. The NIV translation, 'He could bring about no change of mind', is an attempt to tone down the difficulty by suggesting that Esau failed to get his father Isaac to 'repent' of his refusal to bless him, after Jacob had stolen the blessing due to Esau as the firstborn (see the story in Genesis 27). But this is not a correct translation – the author is certainly thinking of Esau's own sins here. That is, after all, the point he wants to make: there are certain sins that leave you with no way back. But why does God seem to close the door like this?

The problem is not as difficult as it seems at first. While I'm disputing translations, I want to disagree with the NRSV as well, which has 'he found no chance to repent.' The Greek literally says, 'he found no place for repentance'. The question we, as interpreters, have to answer is: *where* was there 'no place' for repentance? It can't be *in Isaac*, as we've seen. The other options are *before God*, and *in Esau's own heart*. Surely the latter is correct. We're not talking here about someone who wanted to repent but 'found no chance' to do so because God wouldn't accept it. We're talking about someone who sold his birthright to Jacob his brother in exchange for the first fast-food meal in history (Genesis 25:29–34), someone who is still blaming his brother for his own stupidity. In Genesis 27:36 he says to Isaac, about Jacob, 'He took my birthright.'

But this is just not true. Jacob may have seized an opportunity, but it was Esau who said, 'What good is the birthright to me?' and traded it in for the biblical equivalent of a Big Mac and chips (Genesis 25:32). The biblical judgment is (verse 34), 'So Esau despised his birthright.' Here in Hebrews 12:17 the translation should be, 'He was rejected, because he made no room for repentance in his own heart, even though he sought the blessing with tears.'

This gives us the necessary insight into how our author is using the story of Esau. We have three ingredients here – the seriousness of his sin, the quality of the rest of his life, and his unwillingness to repent – and together these make up a terrible cocktail which deprived him of the 'blessing' he longed for, and will deprive us too if we get into the same situation.

His sin was terribly serious, because it was a rejection of the covenant relationship with God. He knew that, as the firstborn son, he was the bearer of the covenant promises. It was his 'birthright' to live in intimate relationship with God himself, with all the Abrahamic promises ringing in his ears. But he chose to throw it away for a quick meal. This was all in line with the rest of his life – the author calls him 'sexually immoral' and 'godless' (16), and is actually drawing on Jewish tradition here as much as on the stories in Genesis. Esau's wickedness was built up and elaborated in Jewish retelling of the biblical stories. And finally there was no room for repentance in his heart, even though he deeply regretted the effect of his sin on his life, and longed for the blessing that he couldn't now have. What he felt was remorse and self-pity, not repentance and a desire to change.

The author doesn't want his 'Hebrews' to end up like this. He seems especially to fear the hardness of heart (the 'bitter root' of verse 15) that could come to grip them, if they turn away from Jesus. So he warns them, yet again, of the danger of throwing away their confidence (10:35), that is, of rejecting their confident access into an intimate relationship with God through Jesus (10:19), which is now their birthright because they belong to him. There's no suggestion that they might do this for something as trivial as a 'single meal'. But it might be for something as comparatively trivial as freedom from persecution by their fellow Jews or from ostracism by their families. Serious though this would be, it cannot compare to what they would be losing if they threw away Jesus.

So there's no denial of the possibility of second repentance here. If Esau had repented, he would doubtless have been forgiven. The same applies, I think, to Hebrews 6:4–6: so long as people persist in 're-crucifying' Jesus, then there is no space for repentance for them, because repentance no longer leads to the forgiveness of sins apart from faith in Jesus. But if they repent of their hostility towards him, then the story could have a very different ending.

There's considerable insight here into the psychology of sin. The author has reflected on the strange contradiction within Esau: that he could long for the blessing and yet not repent of the action that deprived him of it. He still blames someone else for it. Sin deprives us of self-knowledge, as well as of the knowledge of God.

Probably deliberately, the author has subtly introduced a powerful contrast between Esau in verses 16–17 and Jesus in verses 1–3. They both gave up something in exchange for something else. In both cases it was to do with inheritance. And in both cases it involved their response to pressure from sinners.

▶ Jesus gave up his shame before the cross in exchange for the joy of reaching God's right hand. Esau gave up his relationship with God in exchange for a fast meal.

▶ Jesus became God's heir, sitting at his right hand. Esau lost his birthright as God's heir, the bearer of the Abrahamic promises.

▶ Jesus endured the hatred and hostility of sinners without losing heart. Esau willingly gave in to the trickery of Jacob his brother and became known as a terrible sinner.

So Jesus is the role-model of 'the holiness' without which 'no-one will see the Lord' (14). That holiness can't be gained except through the path of suffering – which means faithful endurance, lasting trust, self-forgetful vision of the invisible Saviour, perseverance in the Father's school, learning to be children like our great Brother.

12:18–24

Smoky mountain, holy hill

A contrast between two mountains brings the whole argument of Hebrews to a suberb climax. Which mountain would you prefer to climb – Sinai or Zion?

What drama here! A wonderful piece of writing, describing and contrasting these two mountains. The simple word 'better' in verse 24 seems to summarize the whole contrast (it's the thirteenth and final time that little word is used in Hebrews). On the one hand is Sinai, grim and threatening, belching smoke and fire, symbolizing death and judgment; on the other is Mount Zion, a beautiful hill with a party already in swing on the summit.

Mount Sinai is described with six fearsome features (18–19) – fire, darkness, gloom, storm, a trumpet blast, and a frightening voice that people can't bear to hear because it is so threatening. The author isn't making this up; he draws his language from Deuteronomy 4:11–12 and Exodus 19:16, from the story of Israel's arrival at Mount Sinai to receive the law. The story of the people's unwillingness to hear God speak comes from Exodus 20:18–19: 'Do not have God speak to us or we will die,' they say. But the whole point was that they had arrived at Sinai precisely in order to hear God's voice, expressing his will for their lives. For the author of Hebrews, there's a terrible paradox here – a tension at the heart of the Old Testament. Just when the people should have been meeting their God face to face, they couldn't bear it. The threat was too great!

Even Moses was frightened for them. His words quoted here (21) are drawn from Deuteronomy 9:19, where he says in full, 'I feared the anger and wrath of the LORD, for he was angry enough with you to destroy you.' He is referring to the making of the golden calf – again, one of the terrible paradoxes of the Old Testament. Immediately after being brought, supposedly, into intimate relationship with their God (Exodus 19:4–6), Israel rebels against him and starts worshipping an idol.

What future can there be in a covenant that starts this way, with terror, resistance, fear and breakdown?

By contrast, Mount Zion is described with eight wonderful features (22–24), in four pairs, which together summarize the whole message of the book. There's a party going on, to which we've been invited; and the author gives us the invitation card, describing where the party is, who's invited, why it's being held, and how to get there.

The where (22a): Mount Zion, city of the living God; the heavenly Jerusalem. This is the city for which Abraham longed, the city built by God which is the real home for his creatures (11:10, 16). This is where his household resides – the 'house' that we are, if we belong to Jesus (3:6). Usually, the expression 'the living God' has a threat built into it, as we've seen in 10:31 and 3:12. It's associated with the threat of Mount Sinai in Deuteronomy 5:26: 'What mortal man has ever heard the voice of the living God speaking out of fire, as we have, and survived?' Under the old covenant, you encounter 'the living God' at terrible risk to your life.

But he is not a threat to those who come to him clutching this particular invitation.

The who (22b–23a): thousands upon thousands of angels in joyful assembly, and the church of the firstborn, whose names are written in heaven. The party is already under way, and the invitation describes who's already there. 'The church of the firstborn' is probably a poetic way of referring to the honours gallery of chapter 11, the 'cloud of witnesses' who cheer us on. They join the angels 'in joyful assembly' – that's putting it mildly! There are many parallels between Hebrews and the book of Revelation, not least this picture of heaven as a place where the angels and the church join in an eternal praise-party.

The why (23b): what's the excuse for this party? The writer speaks of 'God the judge of all, and … the spirits of the righteous made perfect' (NRSV). Such simple words, but so much lies behind them. It's worked! The atonement, the 'purification for sins' that the Son set out to achieve for his Father (1:3), his high-priesthood associated with us in our degradation and death – they've done the job. God, 'the Judge of all', can accept us into his presence as 'righteous', 'made perfect' – a double underlining of the result. With no further barriers, we have 'confidence to enter the Most Holy Place' (10:19). The threat that towered about Mount Sinai and rushed down its slopes, terrifying the onlookers and condemning even animals to death if they got too close, has been wiped away.

The how (24): 'to Jesus the mediator of a new covenant, and to the sprinkled blood that speaks a better word than the blood of Abel'. These are the directions to the party – go by this route, and you can't fail to find it. The author links back to the beginning of the honours list (11:4). Abel's sacrifice was accepted, but his blood cried out to God for justice and vengeance (Genesis 4:10). There was unfinished business there, a terrible crime left unpunished and unatoned for. But Jesus' blood speaks of forgiveness and reconciliation – in fact, he can save us 'completely', because his blood is a constant prayer for our salvation before God (7:25).

'You have not come' (18) … 'you have come …' (22): this is actually the great word 'draw near', which the author also used in his earlier 'invitation' texts, 4:16 and 10:22. It's a worship word, associated with 'approaching' God in the Old Testament. But we now approach, not a literal earthly sanctuary, but its heavenly equivalent, the place where God *really* dwells, and where the angels, the Saviour and the Redeemed are already partying.

Questions

1. Do our worship services look and feel like parties? Do you think they should?
2. Have you replied to this invitation for yourself? Write your own acceptance letter. And don't forget to tell the Lord that you're willing to follow whatever route will lead you up the mountain to the top, facing whatever joys and trials will keep you walking in his footsteps.
3. Do you think that, as new-covenant people, we have definitely 'finished with' the God of thunder and smoke, the God of Sinai? Have we left this idea of God behind, with all its fearfulness and threat, to be replaced by the God and Father of our Lord Jesus Christ, who sends his Son to die for us?

Safe when earth falls

A final warning and exhortation round off the amazing argument of Hebrews. We need to think cosmically, if we are to live in line with this letter.

These verses conclude, not just chapters 11 – 12, but the whole letter. The warning and encouragement here look back both to 10:26–31 and to 2:1–4 – in fact, there are lots of parallels with 2:1–4. The author is bringing us round full circle to where we began.

A vital clue here is unfortunately obscured in the translations. The word 'refuse' in verse 25 is the same as the word translated 'begged' (NIV and NRSV) in verse 19. To bring this out, verse 19 should read something like: 'a voice whose words the hearers *refused* to listen to, begging that not another word be spoken'. And then verse 25 draws the parallel straight across to us. 'Take care – don't *refuse* the one who is speaking to you. For if they didn't escape when they *refused* the one who spoke to them on earth, we certainly won't escape if we reject the one who is speaking to us from heaven.'

This is exactly the contrast we met in 2:1–4. We are now receiving, says the author, a revelation far more significant than Israel received at Mount Sinai. There, angels revealed the law through Moses. But that was 'speaking on earth' compared to what God has now said through his Son! The Son has spoken from heaven – and he continues to do so, through the Holy Spirit. The author is in no doubt: God is still speaking to his 'Hebrews', and he is desperate that they should listen. Don't close your ears, like the Israelites at Sinai – open them to hear what God is saying!

So much is at stake. At Sinai, God's voice 'shook the earth' (26). What will it do next? Verses 26–28 give us some fascinating insight into the author's use of Scripture, and into his theology of the last things, or his *eschatology* (to give it its proper title). The idea of God shaking the earth is quite common in the Old Testament – see for instance Psalms 18:7; 68:8; 77:18; 97:4. It symbolizes his great power, and especially his intervention; he doesn't stay distant, but gets involved, and exercises his power to rescue his people or judge his enemies. 'Shaking the earth' symbolizes such dramatic intervention. But the author has chosen a text from Haggai to make this point, and once again reveals his distinctive approach to the Old Testament. Haggai was used by God to encourage the Israelites, who had just returned from exile in Babylon, to get on and rebuild the temple in Jerusalem. Why are you hanging around? is his message. Great blessings will result if you get on and start building. At the heart of the prophecy stands this encouragement in Haggai 2:6–7 (NRSV): 'For thus says the LORD of hosts: Once again, in a little while, I will shake the heavens and the earth and the sea and the dry land; and I will shake all the nations, so that the treasure of all nations shall come, and I will fill this house with splendour, says the LORD of hosts.'

The author of Hebrews certainly knew that the Haggai passage was about rebuilding the temple in Jerusalem. God promises wonderful things for this new temple. It is going to signal the victory of Israel over all the earth, and the re-establishing of the royal house through Zerubbabel. At last Israel is going to experience the fulfilment of the Abrahamic promise (Genesis 12:1–3); she will be a blessing to the rest of the earth, the heart of the nations, the focus of universal pilgrimage, the source of teaching for the whole world – because God is going to shake the earth and make it happen.

But our author knows too that this never happened, and that Jesus prophesied the final destruction of the temple built in response to Haggai's encouragement (Mark 13). How can Haggai's words be rescued as 'word of God' for today? The author rereads them, and applies them to the rebuilding of earth and heaven by God himself – a reconstruction of the cosmos, which will turn it into a fit habitation for him, a 'kingdom that cannot be shaken' (28). Haggai spoke of more than he understood when he used the words 'once more', because this implies a final, once-for-all act, an unrepeatable 'shaking' of the heaven and the earth, as if a massive earthquake were to destroy and dissolve the entire cosmos – leaving only the kingdom of God. That's the new-covenant equivalent to the shaking of Mount Sinai when God came down to give his law to Israel.

The final dissolution of the universe; the breaking down of the veil between earth and heaven; the appearance of the kingdom of God in all its eternal splendour; and our part in all that. This is what is at stake in the readers' response to 'the voice from heaven'. For we are already 'receiving' this unshakeable kingdom (28). It has not yet arrived in its full glory, but we 'are receiving' it, that is, it is becoming part of our human experience, because the voice from heaven communicates it, 'the powers of the coming age' are already at work among us (6:5), and Jesus our forerunner has already been 'crowned with the glory and honour' (2:9), which mark this new age. The thought of being left out is absolutely horrifying.

How do we avoid being left out? The 'Hebrews' don't have to do very much. Just 'be thankful, and so worship God acceptably with reverence and awe' (28). Very simple, really! Live the life of the new kingdom now, worshipping God 'acceptably'. Just as worship was at the heart of the old covenant, so it is at the heart of the new. But of course, new-covenant worship focuses on Jesus the Son. This is the worship 'acceptable' to God. (The author will say more about this worship in his final chapter.) For God is still 'a consuming fire'. The last words in verse 29 are drawn from Deuteronomy 4:24, the very same passage from which the author drew his terrible description of Mount Sinai in verses 18–19. The same powerful, awesome God rules the universe – the one who thundered and shook the mountain. And one day he will shake the world. Are we ready?

Questions

1. Does this passage frighten you? What do you find especially frightening about it? Is fear (or awe) a good reaction to it (see 'reverence and awe' in verse 28)?
2. Why is giving thanks highlighted here (28)? Do you think that giving thanks is the heart of true worship? How can we make thanksgiving a more real and vibrant focus in our worship?
3. Look back over the last two chapters. The honours list that began with Abel finishes here. What chiefly have you learned from these chapters? What will you take away from them especially?

FIRST THINGS FIRST

Hebrews 13:1-25

Stop and look: What do we do next?

The argument is complete. But what will the Hebrews' response be? The author is on tenterhooks, and clearly wants to see them soon in person (13:19, 23 – he mentions his hope twice). I have no doubt that he would have much preferred to talk all this through with them, rather than write, because it was all so sensitive and tricky. I'm so glad that he wasn't able to see them, and wrote instead!

He deliberately does not discuss directly the vital, nitty-gritty question that arises from his argument: should the 'Hebrews' carry on as members of their synagogue, or not? They knew of many Jewish Christians who had dropped their synagogue membership in favour of worshipping in mixed Jewish–Gentile churches. Is this an implication of the theology of the new covenant that the author teaches?

As we shall see, the closest the author comes to making any comment on this is in 13:13. But it's hardly a direct recommendation. He wants them to work out for themselves, in fellowship with their leaders, and in response to a true view of Jesus and the new covenant, what action they will take. And doubtless he would help them to work it out, when he could talk with them in person.

So in this brief closing chapter he concentrates on giving them basic principles of Christian response to the God of the new covenant: the kind of principles that will help them to work out for themselves what the precise shape of their Christian discipleship will be, in their everyday lives. This is, of course, what makes the chapter useful for us, too! As we'll see, the author focuses on five issues that have central importance for all of us seeking to follow Jesus, whatever our time, place or culture.

The precise issue, whether it's possible for Christians to belong to another religious community as well, is still a live debate in many parts of the world. It's not a question that we can answer in advance, because there are so many factors involved. We need to bear in mind three truths:

1. Christianity is essentially a personal relationship (with God, in Christ, by the Spirit), rather than a religion.

2. Religions and cultures often overlap to a considerable degree, so that it is hard to distinguish where culture ends and religion begins.

3. God appeals deeply to the hearts of all people, so that his voice can be heard in the strangest places.

It's hardly surprising, then, that Christian faith has taken very many different cultural and religious forms, adapting itself to particular places and situations. Today, around the world, for instance, there are many Christian messianic Jewish groups who want to do precisely what the first readers of Hebrews were keen to do – keep their Jewish roots well nourished, and their relationships with fellow Jews open and committed.

What are the basic principles that help us to work out for ourselves what God is calling us to do, wherever we live and whatever our circumstances are? Here's the guidance from the author of Hebrews, in his final chapter.

13:1–8

The bare necessities

What are the absolute essentials of Christian discipleship in any time, any place? Here we get the bare necessities, in eight focused verses.

The author of Hebrews was a superb theologian, giving us the best sort of theology, that ends up in practical discipleship. And here are his five essentials fordistinctive Christian living. As we'll see, he outlines them in 13:1–8, and then expands the same five points in 13:9–25. They all interlink with each other.

First, verses 1–4: *loving relationships*. He focuses on four different sorts of relationship here:

▶ Verse 1: love of each other, basic mutual commitment. 'Keep on loving each other as brothers.' As Jesus said (John 13:35), this is the distinctive mark by which Christians should be identifiable as his followers. Other religions aspire to it, but in the church it should be a reality. If it's not, we might as well pack up and go home.

▶ Verse 2: love of the stranger. The love of the church of Jesus Christ is outward-looking. And it looks outward, not just in order to give, but also in order to receive: to allow others the significance of being angels, messengers of God to us, perhaps very unexpectedly.

▶ Verse 3: love of those who suffer. As we saw above, it involved great social shame to visit and care for prisoners (see on 10:33–34, page 130). The author emphasizes that this is not a reluctant, arm's-length caring, but full association with their pain ('as if you were their fellow prisoners ... as if you yourselves were suffering'), taking on board all their shame as our own.

▶ Verse 4: love within families. Marriage is the heart of family life, and it is at the heart of Christian discipleship that family love should be strong and deep. God takes this very seriously – although of course he's very ready to welcome those who mess up; see 11:31.

These are the essential areas in which Christian love must shine.

Secondly, verse 5: *trust in God for the future*. Again, absolutely basic, and distinctive. On what do we rest our confidence for the future? The world prescribes fat wallets, supplemented by expensive insurance. No – the followers of Jesus Christ put their trust, not in money, but in the unfailing promise of God, given originally to Jacob (Genesis 28:15), then to Israel through Moses (Deuteronomy 31:6, 8), then repeated to Joshua (Joshua 1:5): 'Never will I leave you; never will I forsake you.' It may sometimes *seem* as though he has abandoned us (see 5:7; 12:2), but this Father never abandons his children.

Thirdly, verse 6: *rightly focused worship*. This follows on. If the Lord is shaping all our relationships, and trust in him is framing our future, then worship will flow, as in Psalm 118:6: 'The Lord is my helper; I will not be afraid. What can anyone do to me?' (NRSV). It's interesting that, because of its role in the Passover celebrations, Psalm 118 was probably the psalm mentioned in Matthew 26:30, sung by Jesus and his disciples on their way to Gethsemane. It certainly fits. This is Jesus' worship, facing crucifixion; these words are the vehicle of the faith that brought him through to victory (Hebrews 5:7).

Fourthly, verse 7: *healthy relationships with leaders and with traditions*. It's amazing how much can be packed into one verse. The church cannot exist without good leadership. And good leadership

▶ needs *consent* if it is to succeed, building unity rather than undermining it

▶ works by *example*, inspiring people to follow by going before

▶ is *sensitive to the voice of the Spirit*, becoming God's mouthpiece for the church, and

▶ produces health-giving *traditions* ('Remember …') which nourish the ongoing life of the church.

It's likely that Hebrews is referring here to former leaders who have now died, but whose memory is vital for the community now. They must not be forgotten.

Finally, verse 8: *a 100% focus upon Jesus Christ, beginning, middle and end.* Here's a fascinating observation: Jewish readers (i.e. just Jews) would agree totally with verses 1–6. This is all essential to synagogue faith also. The quotations are all from the Old Testament. What makes it distinctively Christian? The answer is verse 8. And this is really the message of the whole letter: Old Testament faith does not make sense apart from Jesus. But he is the same yesterday, as well as today and tomorrow. He brings all that's best about the readers' Jewish background to completion, or 'perfection' to use the author's own word. He makes sense of their yesterday because he becomes 'the Lord' to whom Psalm 118 refers, the one whom they worship because he secures their future.

Verse 8 is surprising. Why does it appear like this, so suddenly interrupting the chain of instructions? The author has deliberately kept it back for emphasis, because he wants to make sure they've got the point: *Jesus* is now 'the Lord' for us, 'the Lord Jesus Christ', the one who has become the new centre around which Old Testament and Jewish teaching focuses.

Questions

1. Do a little personal and church audit on the four types of relationship in verses 1–4. How do you, and your fellowship, match the author's ideal picture? Is God pointing anything out to you?
2. Verses 5 and 6 suggest that true worship is seriously threatened by wealth. What exactly is the threat? See Jesus' teaching in Matthew 19:23–26. How should we apply this to ourselves today, especially in the wealthy West?
3. How can churches today make sure that they have good leadership, with the hallmarks mentioned in verse 7?
4. You may look back on a long non-Christian past, before becoming a Christian. Can you see how Jesus makes

sense of your 'yesterday'? Or is this yet to be discovered? Share some testimonies around this question.

13:9–25

The real feast

The same five circles of discipleship – interlocking like the Olympic rings – bring this 'word of exhortation' (22) to a powerful conclusion.

The five themes so carefully prepared and laid out in verses 1–8 are now combined and cooked into a final feast. The author shows how the flavours all interact, as he describes 'the altar' at which we can feast (10). We'll look at the themes in the same order as in verses 1–8, but we'll see how they appear interwoven throughout the passage.

First, *loving relationships*. Three of the four sorts of love reappear in this feast. The author illustrates 'brotherly love' in his own attitude to the readers. He calls them 'brothers' in verse 22, and refers to 'our brother Timothy' (23). In the light of such love, the huge labour of producing a letter like this is something truly light (22) – he'd do it again, gladly. The leaders of the community get drawn into this love in verse 24, where 'greet' is literally 'kiss' – so 'greet them lovingly' would be a better translation. In verse 24, too, brotherly love expands beyond their own fellowship. We're bound together in love, across national boundaries. And the leaders base their leadership on love in verse 17, watching anxiously over their flock. Our author has been illustrating this very kind of loving, anxious, watching leadership in his writing. Loveless leaders take no risks, issue unwise challenges, undertake inappropriate labours, keep their own hearts protected.

Love of those who are suffering reappears in verse 16, where it's linked with worship. The worship that truly pleases God is not just heartfelt singing on Sundays, but also passionate service on Mondays – reaching out to people in need.

And *love of the stranger* reappears in verse 9, where it's linked with teaching. Yes, we must be open to 'strangers', and ready to receive them as if they were messengers from God for us (2), but our evaluation of what they say must focus around Jesus. It's possible to be 'carried away by all kinds of strange teachings' (9). And how do we tell? *Grace* is the key – the 'throne of grace' where our high priest has gone before. Does the new message nourish our delight in the grace of Christ? Or does it add *law* – duty, pressure, obligation, religion, rules such as the Jewish food customs?

Secondly, *trust for the future* reappears in the mixture in verses 11–14, and again in verses 20–21. There's no way around suffering in this life. We need a theology that copes well with it, that isn't knocked over when suffering comes because we believed that our heavenly Father was supposed to spare us. And it's a healthy focus on the Son of God that gives us the theology we need. He bore 'disgrace' for us (13), and was rejected by his community, crucified outside the walls of Jerusalem like the Day of Atonement sacrifice he really was (11–12). He did it because he had a vision of where his suffering would lead both him and us (12:3; 2:10). We go that same way – trusting in the city yet to be (14), sitting loose to our earthly home, like Abraham before us (11:9–10), ready to bear the 'disgrace' of Jesus like Moses (11:26).

And what are our resources as we face all this? The final blessing in verses 20–21 tells us that the 'God of peace' can equip us to do his will, whatever the future holds – because he has all the power of the resurrection at his disposal. (Interestingly, this is the only time Hebrews actually mentions the resurrection of Jesus.)

Thirdly, *true worship* appears in verses 9–16, in a very subtle way, as the author summarizes his whole message. The priests of the old covenant ate from the altar – the sacrifices formed their daily food (Levlticus 7:30–36). 'We have an altar from which those who minister at the tabernacle have no right to eat,' he exclaims (10); of course, he means the heavenly altar, to which alone Jesus gives access, and from which we are nourished in our priestly service of him. We are all priests, according to Hebrews, as we saw in 10:19–22. What sacrifices do we offer? Praise (15) – 'the fruit of lips that confess his name' – and practical caring and sharing (16). These are the sacrifices of Christian worship.

Fourthly, *leadership* crops up again, especially in verses 17 and 24, where the author underlines the need for obedience to leaders, but also in verses 18–19, where he underlines the dependence of leaders on those they lead, and their need for openness and accountability. He asks for prayer (18a), tells them about the current state of his own heart and conscience (18b) – how many leaders are truly ready to do this? – and gives the readers a sense of their partnership with him in his work (19).

Finally, of course, *Jesus Christ*. The whole message of the letter is here in a nutshell. God produces what pleases him, now, through Jesus Christ (21) – not through the law, or through his prophets, or through other dramatic interventions. And Jesus Christ is now the one to whom 'glory for ever and ever' is ascribed (21); he becomes a proper object of worship alongside God himself.

This is because of what he has done; he has 'sanctified the people by his own blood' (12, NRSV). We remember how, in the Preface, it was 'after he had made purification for sins' that he was installed as heir at God's right hand (1:3, my translation). His terrible sacrifice, in which he was rejected, tortured and executed like the worst criminal, brings the whole universe back to its creator. His blood is 'the blood of the eternal covenant' (20) because, even though the old covenant is obsolete and ageing and soon to disappear (8:13), the new covenant is not a replacement covenant. It's the old covenant renewed, made 'better', given a 'yesterday' that makes sense, made eternal.

And the loveliest word of all is in verse 20. Previously he was the 'the great high priest' (4:14) or just 'the great priest' (10:21). In case we should feel that this distances him from us – though of course it doesn't; quite the opposite – he now becomes 'the great Shepherd of the sheep'. Shepherds feed and lead, stay close, never leave their flocks, and bring them home. And so he will for us.

Questions

1. How well do we communicate to our churches that worship is not just what we do in services on Sundays, or in other worship gatherings? What exactly is worship?
2. What exactly is 'a theology that copes well with suffering'? How can we acquire it?
3. Here we are at the end of Hebrews! Look back over the whole letter, and register what God has taught you through your study of it. Write it down, and make sure that you share it with others. If you are studying in a group, make sure that you have a 'review' session to do this together.

Further reading

Barclay, William, *Hebrews*, Daily Study Bible (St Andrew Press, 1955)

Brown, Raymond, *The Message of Hebrews: Christ Above All*, The Bible Speaks Today (IVP, 1984)

Hagner, Donald, *Hebrews*, New International Biblical Commentary (Paternoster, 1995)

Hewitt, Thomas, *The Epistle to the Hebrews*, Tyndale New Testament Commentaries (IVP, 1971)

Lane, William L., *Hebrews: A Call to Commitment* (Regent College Publishing, 2004)

Riggans, Walter, *Hebrews*, Focus on the Bible (Christian Focus Publications, 1998)

Wright, Tom, *Hebrews for Everyone* (SPCK, 2003)